The Positive Edge

The First Fundamental to Success

First edition: September 2014

Contents

4

Introduction

This book is about finding the real you, building your self-esteem and strengthening your confidence. It's not about changing, but about discovering who you really are and learning to feel good about it. For years, you've bought into myths and lies about yourself. Today, it's time to break free. Only after you do so can you make the most of your skills, talent and potential while strengthening your self-esteem and confidence.

This book is the launch pad allowing you to introduce an ultimate, dream version of yourself into the reality you live today. It may seem impossible but you can be that idealized person *right now*, if you just believe it's possible and take the right action steps.

No matter what you've been told in the past, you aren't broken or wrong. You are a unique individual, and the most powerful thing you can do for yourself is to learn to appreciate, utilize and love the person you are, from your quirks to your contributions.

There is a single catalyst that can bring about this transformation. It's absolutely the most powerful thing you can do for yourself and will change your life completely. It is to adopt a positive attitude. If it sounds too good to be true, I understand—but becoming a positive person is a proven step toward improving your life and changing your future. Attitude is a huge part of determining what kind of life you'll have. A negative attitude will bring you unhappiness, strife and struggle while a positive attitude brings you to success, consistent fulfillment and unending satisfaction.

A positive attitude isn't just about smiling all the time or trying to convince yourself that you're happy when you're not. It's about creating a strong, stable support system to lift you up and encourage you along the way. It's about depending on yourself by putting a process in place that helps you expand your positive attitude and mindset, sustain it and reinforce it daily.

This isn't just another book that preaches trite advice, clichés and platitudes. I was *inspired* to write this book for you. Sharing what I've learned with others is part of my process to reinforce my own positive attitude daily. This is about more than delivering a message to you; this is about reinforcing my own positivity by helping others join me in feeling the full power of a positive attitude.

My goal is to share all the knowledge I've acquired about how to live a happy, successful, fulfilled life and give you the same positive edge that's allowed me to live the life I've always dreamed of. Honestly, I never saw myself living the life I do now. Only a decade ago I was feeling depressed, I was in debt, and unsure about my future. Now, I'm living a life beyond my wildest dreams. I see now how small my frame of reference was when I used to dream. I couldn't even conceive of the possibilities outside my scope of experience—the amazing people I'd meet and share my life with, the businesses I would build, the opportunities that would come my way—and all of that came because I dared to shift my attitude from negative to positive.

All the elements of the positive edge lifestyle are encapsulated here in bite-sized pieces. I've also developed at least one simple, seven-step program in each section so you can immediately start integrating what you learn into your life. You can think of this book and the programs as your one-stop recipe for success.

My Story

I want you to know that I pass absolutely no judgment at all on people who are struggling. I too have had my fair share of difficulties. We all have our own paths to tread and adversities to overcome.

Every one of us goes through difficult times and experience devastating situations and setbacks. That's part of our human experience, part of our individual journey.

How we choose to see and react to those experiences is the key. We may not be able to change or control them, but within our grasp is the power of choice about how we perceive, react and bounce back. If we can learn to see each of these adversities as an opportunity to learn, grow and challenge ourselves, we can create a three-dimensional experience that helps us build the ultimate model of ourselves, something we could never have done with a one-dimensional, easy life.

My turning point came after my best friend, who happened to be my brother, passed away in a car accident when I was 20 years old. Following that tragedy, my parents' barns burned down and we lost eight horses that had played an important role in our family unit for years. These were hellish nightmares to go through, but they helped inspire me to reach for self-improvement books and programs in order to learn to cope. From books to coaching programs, inspirational texts to motivational products, each one made me a little stronger, more confident and more driven to take control of my life and create my own destiny. I went from being an employee hoping for that next big promotion to building my own million-dollar companies.

So when I talk to you through this book, I'm not just *talking* about the edge that positivity gives you — I'm *living proof* of it.

Life is a series of challenges, problems and obstacles. But it's through these struggles that you become more aware of who you really are. Each is a learning experience allowing you to grow and become a better, more powerful YOU! Having spent close to $200,000 on self-help products, I've seen the good, the bad and the ugly. I have tried things that work and make sense, and things that don't. Most of all, I have seen the results you can get when you find the processes that are a success. I've put everything that I'm teaching to you to use in every area of my life. I'm not here to get rich off selling you some system. This is a compilation of what has worked and continues to work for me personally!

I strongly believe that we're all bigger than the things that happen to us. You can be a victim of circumstance, or you can choose not to be. The decision is yours and must be backed by the actions you take, because it's through action that we show how dedicated we are to becoming our idealized selves. If you allow things to bother you during your day, it will steal your joy and rob you of the ability to become positive and to feel good. If you don't feel good, you can't move forward in life and you will never reach a point of success because you'll never feel that you have. As an added benefit, by feeling good and becoming more positive, you stack the odds of real success (as well as the self-perception of success) in your favor.

Instead, choose not to focus on the obstacles and setbacks. Shine your spotlight instead on what you've gained and learned from each experience.

Opportunity Is Born Of Adversity

If you recognize and appreciate that opportunity arises from adversity, you can move forward positively, with hope, trust and optimism. Many people think that positive thinking is all about putting on rose-colored glasses and pretending that bad things don't happen. But that's not it at all. The positive edge is about focusing on solutions, not problems; about seeing potential, not obstacles; about refocusing your brain to look for answers instead of accepting defeat.

Adversity and resilience need each other. You may at first find them to be strange bedfellows, but together they teach and help us grow. Resilience is also a measure of your potential to bounce back from adversity, which is so important when unforeseen challenges inevitably pop up.

What to Expect as You Read

The Positive Edge was written to inspire your journey toward:

- Increased self-esteem
- The confidence to believe in yourself and do what makes you happy
- Unlocking the truth about what you want to create
- Discovering the perfect way to achieve all you desire
- The ability to see the steps you've already taken toward success
- The power to coach yourself through difficult times and stay positive through adversity

Preparing for your journey is a process focused on switching gears into the mindset and "heartset" that you're worthy, lovable and have a valuable identity.

Once you reach this point, you'll no longer allow the craziness of life to defeat you. All the ups, downs, problems, obstacles and negative stuff will slide off you like water off a duck so you can continue on to being the best you can be.

In my work in the insurance and investment industry, as a certified life coach and as a motivational speaker, I've helped many people who've had low self-esteem. Together, we were able to increase their confidence and self-image and evolve their negative attitude to a positive mindset.

My key aim was to get those people to stop seeing negative experiences as something that tore them down, but instead see them as opportunities to build from, using the power they already possessed. I wanted to show them that with their own inner strength and a dose of determination, they could rely on themselves, take charge and turn their lives around. In this book, I do the same for you. I'm also committed to helping you gain a greater understanding of yourself and your circumstances, to learn good coping skills and to strengthen yourself so that you can bounce back from any circumstance you face.

Once you learn these powerful lessons, the positive experiences you have will easily and naturally escalate in number and frequency and gain a momentum of their own, much like a snowball rolling downhill gets larger and larger simply as a result of its own momentum.

Success and happiness in all aspects of life don't occur by accident or coincidence. The more positive you are, the more good things will flow more effortlessly. But first, you must learn to be the snowball and roll with it.

The Tools You Need to Get Started

The most important tool for this journey is an open mind. In addition to that, you will need:

- **The Victory Journal:** The Victory Journal is a very powerful resource that demonstrates, in real time, the importance of acknowledging and writing down your victories or wins each day. When you see them written down, you'll finally realize you made more progress than you thought. This helps you find something to feel grateful for and increases your confidence, both of which make you more positive. It works a lot like compound interest; each day, your past victories build up the inspiration you feel to be more hopeful, confident and optimistic.

So many people think they've had a really rough day and wallow in the funk of it. Maybe they have had a rough day, or maybe that's just the way they've chosen to perceive the day. Remember—your perception of reality is always a choice. But if you reflect, recognize and record your small victories, you come to realize that your day wasn't so bad after all, a realization that instantly switches your focus to the positive and what you actually achieved.

I want the Victory Journal to become part of your daily arsenal—a go-to weapon in your bag of tricks. Think of it as a tool that helps you feel better about yourself, your progress and your achievements at any time. When you witness and realize its power, you won't want to put it down.

Remember, the goal of the journal is to celebrate all your wins—not just the major ones. That means an entry could be something very simple, such as:

"Today I made a phone call I didn't want to make, and felt nervous about, but it all worked out fine. Even better than I thought. And now I feel I can do another, and feel better about it, and I'll do better."

Or it could be something else, such as:

- "I had that overdue conversation with a friend and set my boundaries with them. I said NO, with strength and certainty. I said it firmly, gently and kindly, without any doubt."
- "I got around to organizing my paperwork for my taxes, and I feel so much better."
- "I cleaned the front garden."
- "I tidied up the garage and did a huge clean-out."

The goal of your entries is not to impress anyone or to be worthy of the history books, but to reinforce your positive attitude, raise your energy and help you build momentum for the following day. It's all about giving positivity an advantage in your life—no matter how small. Just a slightly higher level of positive energy over negative energy can be enough to catapult you into new opportunities, and your journal can be the tool to help you get that edge.

It's amazing all the changes the journal will make you feel. You'll find yourself hungry for more wins, a feeling that will push you to work harder and go after more. If you're at all competitive with yourself, you'll want each day's wins to beat out the last—and that means you'll be conquering your fears and increasing your personal and professional successes.

- **Workbook:** The companion workbook provides complementary exercises that you can work on while you read this book or after. These exercises can be done for years to come in order to refresh and recharge your positive edge.

- **Seven-Steps Workbook:** Within this book are seven-step exercises in every section to help effect change in your life and get you on track to developing a more positive attitude and habits. I've also broken out these steps into a separate workbook of its own so you have a safe space to do the exercises, write down your thoughts and really dig deep into making changes. Like the workbook, the seven-step book can be redone year after year to keep your positive edge intact.

- **The Gratitude Journal:** One way to make sure you stay positive is to focus on all the amazing things that happen to you each day. That's exactly what the Gratitude Journal helps you do. It allows you the space to write down everything you're grateful for each day. And it doesn't have to be big stuff—you can write down the little things that often go unnoticed but for which you are grateful. This will increase your positivity and put you in the perfect mindset for the Positive Edge system to work.

All right, that's enough talking—let's get to work.

Chapter 1:
Laying the Foundation

Gaining the positive edge isn't just about the internal changes you must make to be a more positive person; it's also about creating a supportive environment around you that encourages you and stacks your odds in favor of success. To make this a way of life, you must have a regimen of success principles, methods, tools, habits and routines in place to support you in strengthening and sustaining your new thinking. This foundation is established through your efforts and then begins to take on a life of its own. Remember that snowball we talked about in the last chapter? This is when it starts rolling and collecting new flakes to itself.

Four Aspects of the Edge

Everything you need to do in order to develop the positive edge is broken down into four aspects of your being:

- Thoughts: These are both conscious and subconscious beliefs, reflections, ideas and habits. Controlling your thoughts and changing them creates a domino effect that brings positivity to the other three aspects.

- Energy: Your energy is the palpable vibration that you send off—whether you know it or not. This energy feeds into the dynamics discussed in the law of attraction and acts like a magnet bringing back exactly what you put out.

- Emotions: Your emotions are your feelings about events, people and situations in your life. But your emotions don't just revolve around things outside of you; they also reflect your self-esteem and confidence.

- Attitude: The attitude you have dictates your outlook on life. It's either positive or negative, optimistic or pessimistic. In order to gain the positive edge, there can be no straddling the attitude fence. You must commit to the dark or the light.

The positive edge cannot be gained by paying attention to only one of the four aspects. All four must work in concert to create an overwhelming positive energy source within you that extends out and affects everyone and everything you come in contact with. You must be ready to overhaul each of these four parts of yourself to gain the full power of the positive edge.

When I talk about concepts affecting your thoughts, I'll use this icon:

This icon will represent concepts that involve your energy:

This icon will represent concepts that affect your attitudes:

And finally, this icon will represent concepts related to your emotions:

How Thoughts Become Things

 Our thoughts have an undeniable power: they create our reality. They generate the emotions and feelings that create the energy vibration levels around us.

Thoughts, emotions and feelings are energy systems. The energy our thoughts and emotions create generates further energy. Our thoughts and their energy then become things that materialize or manifest in our lives.

We can choose to send our thoughts along a constructive path up Optimistic Road, Constructive Avenue and Positive Street or down Destructive Lane and Negative Trail.

This is not imaginary hoo-hah. It's based on scientific fact and quantum physics. It's been covered in *law of attraction* literature and discussions.

I'm sure you've heard statements such as:

In 1994 doctor of alternative medicine Masaru Emoto began freezing water and examining it under a microscope. After experimenting with every kind of water, from tap water to lake and river water, rural and urban water sources, he found that the beauty of the frozen water crystals were not impacted by the quality or type of water he studied. Instead, they were affected by the way the water was treated before it was frozen.

He found that saying, thinking and doing positive things such as offering prayers for the water, showing it happy pictures and saying nice things to it before freezing it would result in the formation of beautiful, snowflake-like crystals.

If positive energy and thoughts can do this to water, imagine what it can do for you!

- What we think about, we bring about.

- You are what you think about most.

- Where attention goes, energy flows—or—energy flows where attention goes.

- Whatever you believe you can achieve, you can attain.

So, if thoughts are things, what do you think will happen if you don't take control of the thoughts you have and change them?

I'll tell you what—absolutely nothing. Your life will remain the same, full of ruts, sadness and disappointment.

Some people see opportunity in everything that happens to them. A car accident, to these fortunate souls, may be an inconvenience or expense—but it's also an opportunity to meet another driver and network with them. It's a reminder to review their insurance policy and a prompt to slow down, smell the flowers and enjoy life. Others see only obstacles and adversity. You can be a victim of your circumstances or you can create your circumstances by changing your thinking and then taking action.

 An Inventory of Your Thoughts in Seven Steps

1. Be aware of your thoughts. Then be aware of your energy.

2. Monitor your internal language and the dialogue you have within your head.

3. Write down your thought and word patterns, or *word tracks*.

4. Identify the thoughts that don't serve you and those that do.

5. Eliminate the negative words. Every time a negative thought enters your mind, immediately replace it with a positive

thought. It's helpful if you prepare beforehand and preselect two or three positive thought experiences that really make you feel good, even fabulous. Reach for these at the moment you need them rather than trying to find one when you're in a stressed place, as that's not likely to bring about the result you need and desire.

6. For example, let's say you make an error on some paperwork. When you discover the error, your word tracks likely send down some negative phrase that you're used to telling yourself, such as, "I'm so stupid! I should've caught that!" As you catch your brain "saying" those negative words, stop yourself and say, "You know what? This is a great opportunity for me to figure out why I missed that and strengthen my concentration skills so it doesn't happen again." Or, instead, you could remind yourself of something great you did.

7. Do this exercise for a day. Then do it for a week, and then a month. Eventually, you'll create the habit of not allowing negative thoughts to overcome you. By transforming them into opportunities to be positive, you boost your self-esteem and create an overall positive attitude and self-image.

Write down your victories and wins and the progress you made that day in your Victory Journal.

Change Your Life by Changing Your Beliefs and Thoughts

 What is reality? It's how you choose to see, look at and interpret the information presented to you each day. This information passes through the filter of your eyes, your beliefs, your experiences and your attitude before hitting your subconscious for assessment.

A person can see only one version of reality at a time, but can easily slide into another version during the next because reality isn't made of concrete. Two people can see the same version of reality in very different ways because much of our reality is centered around how we perceive things. Controlling the version you see ensures that you stay positive and motivated. To do this, you must adjust the way you process information. That can heavily depend on your personality, which is the sum total of your character and is driven by your beliefs and thoughts.

Some people believe that your personality is set by the age of seven, and that once it develops, it won't change. The argument goes that by your teens, or your 20s, your capacity for change is limited, possibly even nonexistent.

That's simply not true. If it were, change could never be possible. You can create your life based on your beliefs and thoughts, and direct it to become an answer to your greatest desires.

Your Conscious and Subconscious Minds

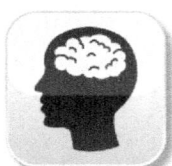 First up, let's start by gaining a basic understanding of the conscious and subconscious minds. It's essential to distinguish between how differently both minds operate, particularly since the latter is so difficult to understand and can be at the root of self-sabotage.

Your Conscious Mind

Your conscious mind operates on an external, outside-world level. You can see its influence tangibly and concretely, and you're "consciously" aware of it.

Well … most of the time. There's one exception that occurs when we choose to interpret reality differently than it actually is. This influences your perceptions, imposes illusions (whether true or false) and changes the way you see things.

Your conscious mind is aligned with your left brain, which handles analysis and calculation. This is where goals are set, action is taken, and progress is measured against preset criteria.

Essentially, your conscious brain is represented by the decisions you make and the actions you take. It analyzes the data of experiences you've had and comes to a realization or decision that you're always aware of.

Your Subconscious Mind

Your subconscious mind operates on an inner level. It's also more aligned with your right brain, which is where ideas, inspirations, purpose and passions originate. It's also where your intuition and gut instinct come from—when they surface, you can listen to, follow and make them work for you.

As you can see, the subconscious may be invisible, but it's a powerful part of who you are and what you become. Mastering it is vital to creating a positive edge lifestyle.

You may consciously think to yourself, "Of course I want success!" But lurking underneath that thought are subconscious forces sabotaging your progress.

That's because your subconscious is at work to protect you by keeping you safe within your comfort zone, maintaining the status quo—so you never feel that grave sense of disappointment that comes with failure.

The subconscious doesn't understand that it may be preventing you from achieving the success that you want and desire, but it will once you put a stop to it.

 ## Understanding Your Conscious and Subconscious in Seven Steps

1. Write down several examples of your conscious mind at work. This can include things such as deciding what to wear to work or eat for dinner.

2. Write down several examples of your subconscious mind at work. Since we don't generally know what our subconscious is doing when it's doing it, these are likely to be hindsight examples of times you've sabotaged your own success, lost confidence or talked yourself out of trying something. Traces of your subconscious can also be found in patterns of behavior.

3. Write down the differences between your conscious thought results and the subconscious thought results.

4. What are some subconscious actions that you could've prevented with conscious thought?

5. Let's explore how powerful your subconscious really is. Write down some of the times you've done something that, on paper, shouldn't have been possible.

6. How might your subconscious have played a role in accomplishing these "impossible" things?

7. Write a list of the things you want to retrain your subconscious on. Next to each topic, write down an affirmation you can use to help steer your subconscious.

The Universal Law of Attraction

 The law of attraction is a force of nature that philosophers such as Plato have been discussing for millennia. Through study, we know that the concept has actually been around since the beginning of time. It's not something humans made up. Instead, it's a natural phenomenon on par with the laws of gravity and cause and effect.

The theory behind the law of attraction is based in the science of quantum physics (also referred to as quantum mechanics), which is the study of motion and subatomic particles that explain how energy works. This is important since our world is made up of energy vibrations and interactions that have a great effect on our personal and global experience.

On a basic level, the law of attraction has two key irrefutable principles:

1. The way you focus your energy determines what energies are focused on you. In other words, what you focus most of your time thinking about is what you attract to yourself, whether positive or negative.

2. The law can be used to manipulate the kind of energy you bring to yourself. By consciously focusing on positive energy, you can influence the law of attraction to bring you that very thing.

Everything in our universe is made up of energy. Both humans and inanimate objects emit energy waves. There is a constant universal flow of energy back and forth. It vibrates and fluctuates, high and low.

Energy waves are invisible to the eye, but imagine if they were visible, like in your own special-effects-heavy movie, you would see energy waves of varying intensity emanating from everything around you.

Law of attraction principles dictate that you'll attract like energy to what you put out there. This means you can become what you believe and manifest whatever it is you spend most of your time focusing on. You can successfully channel energy into productive relationships and activities that bring great results. Likewise, your energy can be confused and block what you desire most.

If you're not clear on what you want, you'll send conflicting messages and energies and find yourself stuck and achieving counterproductive results.

Law of Attraction History

Law of attraction principles appear throughout time in philosophies and writings, including those of Plato. In historical science texts, it was known as the *law of affinity*. It was defined as *like tending toward like*.

The law of attraction is also covered in early 20th-century literature, including in Napoleon Hill's *Think and Grow Rich*,

Wallace D. Wattles' *Science of Getting Rich*, James Allen's *As a Man Thinketh* and many others.

More recently it was extensively covered in *The Secret* book and movie by Rhonda Byrne. Other modern-day law of attraction experts include Mark Victor Hansen, Jack Canfield, Neale Donald Walsch, Esther Hicks, Bob Proctor, John Assaraf, Dr. Joe Vitale, Natalie Ledwell and Marci Shimoff.

If you understand the principles of the law, it can give you new insight into your life. It can help explain the events of your past and help you raise your awareness of the present. This, in turn, will allow you the power to reprogram your mind to create change in the future. In short, by understanding the law, you can positively adjust the course of your life and the quality of your experiences.

The ultimate goal in learning about the law isn't just to explain why your life is where it is today; it's to determine the best way to improve your life going forward. The key message for you is: You can attract into your life whatever you want, if you know how to understand and apply these principles.

How Success Gains Momentum

One of the ways you can help yourself become that snowball, growing larger and larger as it rolls downhill, is by writing down your daily victories, even the tiny ones. When you do, you focus on the positive and allow the law of attraction to help your successes gain momentum and compound. Eventually, this positive focus becomes an automatic habit you don't have to think about. This will impact all areas of your life: relationships, health, career and more.

In the beginning especially, the journal helps you effectively and practically focus on the positive, boost your attitude, appreciate your results, increase your self-esteem and drive your thought focus toward happiness and success.

For example, take someone who doesn't have much confidence about public speaking. As this person continues to record small victories every day, she becomes more confident, then even more confident, and eventually she overcomes her fears.

Maybe she starts out by challenging herself to do a short, one-minute presentation at a small department meeting. After recording the win, she feels emboldened and progresses to a three-minute standing presentation at the next company-wide meeting. That win gives her even more confidence, and she schedules herself a 15-minute presentation at a convention. By this process, she gains more confidence and, like gravity helps a falling apple reach the ground, the law of attraction helps her confidence build.

With Victories, Size Doesn't Matter

It's important to count your victories no matter how small. Add everything up in your life and keep an inventory of the wins.

Some victories are hidden within situations that, on the surface, don't make you feel very victorious. Perhaps you made a mistake and learned a lesson that showed you the right next step to take. Or a seemingly insignificant event led to a significant insight that helped you break through or move forward.

These are huge wins and gaining the positive edge is all about acknowledging them so that you may appreciate all the ways you're winning. Often it's a matter of perspective. You can choose to look at life events as wins, or you can choose to see them as losses, but only by seeing them as wins will they serve to benefit you and will they help make your attitude more positive.

 The Victory Journal in Seven Steps

1. Commit to recording victories and wins in your Victory Journal each and every day.

2. On the first day, pick just one or two tiny victories. The goal is to create your new habit and begin compounding its positive benefits (or, if you prefer, sending that snowball down the hill). If you forget to do it for a day, get yourself back on track the next.

3. Be grateful for the small victories. Appreciation is vital to the process, so be grateful for what you have and appreciate your victories, big or small. You might think that gratitude is something only to be practiced when times are good, but that's not the case. When you can find ways to be grateful in bad times, you gain a tremendous amount of power, immediately shifting your circumstances. This helps ensure that you learn the right lessons to completely change your future.

4. Do a big-picture inventory of the victories in your life so far. Include the lessons you've learned and the ways these wins changed your life. This self-reflection brings clarity and makes you appreciate what you've achieved with your special gifts and talents.

5. Set aside a specific time each day to record your victories. You only need a couple of minutes, although you can take as long as you like. This is your special time; allow it to fit your personal needs.

6. Divide your Victory Journal into sections:

- Top five victories for the day
- Milestone victories achieved over a predetermined period of time
- Goals
- Action plan
- Ideas, the perfect place to record ideas and inspirations
- Life purpose and passion
- Description of your ideal future self
- Notes and observations

- Miscellaneous, which is a space for anything else you'd like to note down along your journey

7. Finally, do whatever it takes to make writing in your Victory Journal a daily habit.

Why You Should Start Journaling Today

 I've mentioned journaling a few times now. Those of you who've never kept a journal or diary might be wondering why. So let's take a moment to consider the powerful impact of developing a journaling habit.

Successful people have a process of writing things down that helps them be what they are—successful. They write down their goals and their progress against achieving those goals. They have a very clear picture at all times of how they're progressing and they make notes about what is and isn't working so they can adjust their approach. All of this helps them to see what's moving them closer to their goals and what's taking them further away. These observations facilitate tweaks and changes so that the individual can redirect toward better results and outcomes. You know what this is? It's journaling, even if they don't call it that.

Seeing all of your goals, plans and accomplishments written down stimulates both your cognitive and visual capacities. This helps you to visualize the ideal life you want to create and *are creating* as you journal.

Noting your activities and insights and keeping track of them serves to constantly keep you focused on your goals and the progress you're making toward them. Your journal enables you to see a detailed snapshot of the actions you're taking, changes you're experiencing and anywhere you're coming up short or not holding yourself accountable. Without the journal, you might not see any of these things.

Journals aren't just for tracking goals and progress; they're also great for tracking ideas. I keep one with me 24/7 so that I can write down any idea that comes to mind. Later, I review the notes I've made and determine which are worth exploring further, which should wait and which don't really fit my purpose.

Noted motivational speaker Zig Ziglar once described two test groups of top sales teams. One group kept thorough written records of their activities, including exactly what they were achieving and the outcomes of their activities.

The other group didn't keep any written records of their activity. When they looked at the sales results of both teams over the test period, there was a very noticeable difference. The group that kept good records not only hit their targets but also exceeded them.

The group that did not keep written records didn't come close to reaching their targets. They were sure they were hitting their targets, but because they didn't have anything in writing, they couldn't see how far from the mark they really were.

Another big benefit of keeping a journal is that it helps build confidence and self-esteem by providing factual evidence of success. This reaffirms the positive benefits and outcomes as you get closer to realizing your goals.

Journaling in this focused way really helps to paint the picture of who you're becoming every day and what you can achieve.

"Keeping a journal will absolutely change your life in ways you've never imagined."

— Oprah Winfrey

Chapter 2:
The Joy Principle

 When was the last time you felt pure joy? Maybe you've never felt it at all. You will now, though, because it's a vital component to the positive edge. With joy, that extreme and pure expression of happiness, you give extra power to your positivity snowball. So much so, it grows exponentially. Best of all, like money in a savings account, its returns compound; not only will you find joy in the experience of the feeling itself but you'll also get even more joy as you gain the benefits of the positivity that bounce back to you.

The Power of Feeling Good

Learning how to feel good is one of the most important things you can do for your life. It's also the one thing you must get right in order to move forward in your career. It's a simple concept, but not always easy to master.

When you feel good, uplifted and motivated, you're excited and optimistic. There's nothing in life that can't be accomplished when you feel this way. Even more important, there's nothing of value in life that can be accomplished when you **don't** feel this way. The influence of positive energy on a person, especially that which comes from joy, is immense.

But the power of joy isn't just found in how it makes you feel but in what it makes you *do*. Positive energy and the joy that extends from it make you a better leader. These feelings change how you treat others so that they're more likely to trust you, more devoted to your success and more likely to feel valued by you. When you make your friends, associates and employees feel valued, you make them want to work harder. You set a bar for them that they want nothing more than to reach.

Joy and Relationships

Your working relationships aren't the only ones that benefit from feeling joy. I've never met a married couple devoted to sharing regular moments of joy who later ended up divorcing. When you invest the time in your relationships to experience joy together, you create an unbreakable bond that can strengthen even the shakiest connection.

We've spoken a lot about the positivity snowball, so now let's talk about a positivity scrapbook. People who don't focus on sharing moments of joy with their friends and loved ones will have a spotty memory book. In other words, when they look back on the time they spent with others, they may see some good times but they may also see a lot of bad or indifferent times.

But those who make an active effort to share joy with the people they care about will have a memory book filled with laughter, happiness and power. Likewise, their Victory Journal will be filled with wins. Much like the positivity snowball, this will bring more positive feelings and actions into the relationship, which feeds into the feeling of joy, creates even stronger memories and allows the relationship to develop into something that's unbelievably strong and requires little effort to maintain.

Think back to the last challenge you faced in your relationship with your spouse. Perhaps it was related to money, or maybe it was influenced by family stresses or other difficult situations. How much easier would it have been to get through those difficult times if you'd had a foundation of joyful memories to look back on and, more importantly, to look forward to? Does that sound weird—to look forward to memories? If you're in the habit of *making* memories with the people you love, then you'll understand that memories aren't always tied to the past. They're active inventions you invest your time in creating, which means you can look forward to making new ones for the rest of your life.

Joy and Health

Have you noticed that there are never any popular, viral videos on the Internet about miserable, sick, unhappy elderly people? But there are many showing elderly people taking the time to feel joy. They dance, they sing, they laugh, they joke. Joy is the original fountain of youth. It's an elixir of health. A study conducted by Brigham Young University found that even the discussion of positive experiences led participants to increased well-being, more energy and overall life satisfaction.

Feeling joy is one of the simplest things you can do to improve all aspects of your life. Many recent studies have shown that pets can help improve health and reduce chronic issues such as high blood pressure. Do you think that's because the purring of a cat has the physical power to change your blood pressure, or do you think that the joy of having a happy cat or dog around improves your overall well-being?

The Power of the "Compounding" Effect on Making Changes in Your Life

There's absolutely no denying that a snowball gets bigger as it rolls downhill. This is a great illustration of the power of a compounding effect. This compounding effect also works on your successes and your positive energies. It intensifies your efforts, has a multiplying impact and gains a forward momentum all its own.

Positive habits, when practiced consistently, gain the benefit and power of the compounding effect. Repetition creates new neural pathways in your brain and instills new habits that then become part of your normal behavior.

As time goes on, you'll find that you don't have to think about being positive or make an effort to be—it will happen automatically. This is empowering.

As you practice these new habits consistently, they build upon each other and multiply, giving you an exponential effect that creates momentum and further growth in the direction you desire.

 ## *Feeling Joy in Seven Steps*

It almost seems wrong that it should be so easy to feel such a powerful and life-changing emotion, but the truth is feeling joy is so simple, you can do it right now.

1. Think of someone who makes you happy. This can be someone you love or it can be your favorite comedian, a friend or a coworker who always cheers you up. It can even be a pet. Get a good mental picture of the person (or animal) and think about the things that they say or do when they cheer you up.

2. Spend time developing a "happy place" you can visit in your mind at any moment. It could be a sunny picnic spot in a field of heather or a cool, shady, moss-covered rock next to a babbling stream. Just create a clear concept of a place that makes you feel joy whenever you think of it and then go there whenever you need a happiness boost.

3. Create more positive habits. The more positive you are, the happier you'll be and the more joy you'll experience during your day. Build this habit of positivity by using the exercises in Chapter 4.

4. Spend more time with people you love. Often, it's the special people in our lives who bring us the most joy. Make a weekly or monthly date to spend time with the individuals you most enjoy seeing.

5. Do volunteer work. There is a certain kind of lasting joy that comes from helping others. Dedicate some time to directly helping organizations that matter to you.

6. Spend time with animals and children. The purest expressions of joy often come from spending time with children and animals—both of which are very pure, innocent and fun. Enjoy their antics, sense of wonder and process of discovery.

7. Play. Just because you're "grown up" doesn't mean you can't enjoy playing. From Frisbee in the park to board games

on family night, playing is fun and gives an immediate spike of joy.

Chapter 3:

Overcoming Obstacles

Let's cover some of the things that keep you stuck and unhappy, preventing you from succeeding.

Blockages, Barriers and Obstacles

 In life, we all find blockages, barriers and obstacles (BBOs) interrupting our progress and waylaying our chance at success. Do you want to know what's going to be one of your biggest BBOs?

Look in the mirror … it's you and your mindset.

I'm not trying to be unkind, but this is the cold, hard truth. In telling you this, I'm trying to help you be realistic so that you have a better chance of recognizing self-sabotage and taking responsibility for it. Only after doing so can you gain the power to change your situation.

There's a fundamental thought buzzing around inside each of us. It never stops, although it's usually far below conscious awareness. This buzzing is the summary of everything we believe about ourselves. It's like a never-ending news feed of information all about the person we believe we are. The buzz will be different for each of us, though there are only a few variations around the central theme of *not being good enough.*

Once you realize that this is the message your subconscious spews when you let it run on autopilot, you can take steps to reprogram the message, replacing it with a new, positive thought that truly serves you. Trust me, this is one of the most powerful and healing things you can do for yourself.

Look at your life. Identify the recurring emotional states that you endure. Those emotional pits—the dark days filled with angst and self-doubt, the moments when you refuse to believe anything good about yourself—those are not yours. You're experiencing them, but you do not own them. They come from a lifetime of thoughtless habit that doesn't rely one single ounce on conscious thoughts about the reality of you.

Have you ever wondered what's holding you back from achieving all you want in life, all that you know you desire and deserve? It's this subconscious thought pattern—which is why you must reprogram it. Finding and replacing mine was one of the most powerful, life-healing events I have ever experienced.

Self-Limiting, Negative Beliefs

Your personal self-limiting beliefs can sabotage not only your income but also your relationships, career, business, health and fitness in ways you're probably not aware of.

Did you know that the simple act of acknowledging that you have limiting beliefs gives them power? The thing is, when you focus on your limiting beliefs as a way of putting boundaries on what you can reasonably hope to accomplish, you allow those limits to sink their hooks into you and take control. You give them ultimate power over your life and they clearly dictate what you can and can't do. Yet, these are just beliefs—they're nothing more than thoughts you have about the potential you hold. And just like any negative thought, they can be stamped out and transformed in the blink of an eye.

The subject of self-limiting beliefs is one I'm passionate about because I believe it's at the crux of your problems with finding success in life. These beliefs and thoughts determine why you may be grappling with self-esteem issues and why you aren't living the life you most want.

Beliefs: You Are What You Think About Most

 If you're like I was when I first discovered this truth, then you probably have a lot of questions. Where do these beliefs come from? How are they formed? Why do we hang on to them? How do we reprogram them? Let me try to answer these questions.

A belief is something you repeat internally until you unquestionably accept it as truth. Self-limiting beliefs are negative thought patterns formed around our self-worth, relationships, money, body image, fitness and so on.

These beliefs are rooted in your subconscious mind. Without a doubt, these beliefs are responsible for the great majority of the results you see in your life. They really do have that much power in forming your reality.

You probably have a lot of examples of times when you've wanted something—wanted it badly, and not gotten it. You might be wondering how this can happen when it flies in the face of the law of attraction. But the law of attraction only works if there's no pushback happening within you. If, on a subconscious level, you still believe that it's not possible for you to achieve the thing you want, your self-limiting beliefs will interrupt the positive energies your conscious mind tries to send. The law of attraction cannot work with this kind of interference.

If you haven't yet achieved what you want in life, it's highly likely that you have a self-limiting belief that blinds you to those opportunities that would otherwise help you make these dreams reality.

Your subconscious is the real powerhouse in your mind. It's significantly more powerful than your conscious mind as its programming overrides your conscious thought. Imagine it this way—your conscious thoughts are like a costume you put on. Sure, you may resemble the character you've dressed up as—but underneath, you are still *you*. When you try to don a conscious thought without overriding the unconscious beliefs you have, you're just putting on a costume and that's not going to fool the law of attraction into giving you what you want.

It's not all about the law of attraction and energy, however. When self-limiting beliefs exist below the surface, they compel you to act in certain ways that sabotage your life and capacity for success. Think about the last time you turned down a perfectly great opportunity due to fear. The last time you talked yourself out of doing something that could have helped you reach your goal. That's sabotage, and the saboteur is you.

The Creation of Self-Limiting Beliefs

Our beliefs are formed in early childhood. We pick them up from the experiences we go through as well as the adults around us. Parents, caregivers, teachers, television shows, books, newspapers and more communicate these limits.

These messages can be about many different things, such as who you are in the world, what you are or aren't capable of being and achieving, what you're worth, what you should think about your body, and so on.

Most of these messages nestle in your mind before you reach the age of six. The limits can be embedded into our minds before we're old enough to question their legitimacy. Like a sponge, you absorb as fact everything you see, feel and hear around you, whether good or bad. Because you're a child, you have no capacity to understand the events and people or to sort through their messages and assess their accuracy.

You don't have filters in place yet for screening, questioning or judging the information you absorb. It goes straight in, and after just a little bit of repetition, the messages are embedded into your subconscious.

Even hearing your parents fighting about an issue will create the opportunity to absorb what's happening and to understand the statements made as fact. Think about how many children grow up watching their parents fight about money. You might wonder how this affects their subconscious thoughts about finances. Sadly, it implants the self-limiting belief that money is bad and causes arguments and conflict. This then becomes an extremely difficult message to override.

Not all self-limiting beliefs are gained in childhood. Some are formed through your own unique adult experiences. Your perception of these experiences, already colored by subconscious negativity, becomes invisible to your criticisms and judgments because they fit into the self-limiting belief mold you gained as child. A friend's or partner's betrayal, a difficult situation at work, a presentation that didn't go well, family members who turn on you—all of these can be wounding experiences that you believe you deserve, even if you didn't.

Most people don't realize that the majority of their self-limiting, negative beliefs are not actually accurate assessments of their capabilities or potential. They only become true because we've subconsciously decided they are.

Once you reach adulthood, it becomes your responsibility to identify, recognize and reformat embedded thoughts in order to control the course of your life. As you age and gain more life experience, you become capable of judging, questioning, critically analyzing and comparing things rather than blindly absorbing everything you experience. Your brain begins to filter what comes in to see whether it makes sense for you. Of course, by then, your long-embedded, self-limiting beliefs have a grip on your worldview and you don't even know that they're there. It's likely they've already been causing chaos, blocking success in different areas of your life. So even though you now have the capacity to crush them, you can't battle an enemy you don't know exists.

Beliefs are formed through repeated patterns of thinking. Like a lint ball hiding under the bed, they roll around in your head collecting more and more negativity. The primary reason they hold importance, power and meaning for you is because you've chosen to believe that these thoughts are true, based on your perceptions. By allowing yourself to hold onto these beliefs, you also hang onto the limitations they impose. You could just as easily let positive thoughts and affirmations be the tools that create your patterns of thinking if you focus on letting go of the negative, self-limiting beliefs. Instead, repeat your affirmations, re-read your Victory Journal or simply say nice things to yourself.

Some examples of self-limiting beliefs include:

- I'm not good enough.

- I'm not deserving of anything.

- There's never enough for me to get a share.

- I'll never be able to work hard enough to get money.

- Abundance is not for me.

- Things don't come to me easily.

- Other people have all the luck.

Self-limiting beliefs like these take root in your subconscious mind and block your success. No matter how hard you work, you will not succeed with these thought saboteurs hitching a ride in your life.

Focusing on the Positive

If your mental soundtrack includes a lot of self-limiting statements, there's one simple thing you can do to distract yourself from this negativity and get back on a positive track. Best of all, it's simple and fun.

All you have to do is overwhelm the negativity with positivity directed at yourself. When the loop of limiting thoughts starts playing in your mind, start thinking about all the amazing, positive traits you have. Shout them over the sound of the negative voice. Think about things like:

- Your desires
- Your strengths
- Your skills
- Your good health
- Your accomplishments
- Your hobbies
- Your passions

The goal here is to focus on all the *un*limited joy you can derive out of other facets of your life and to revel in it. Eventually, this will eclipse the negative and put you in the right state of mind to start receiving positive life messages that help you on your trek to your goals.

Reprogramming Your Self-Limiting Beliefs

While the last section discussed a quick fix for your self-limiting beliefs, it's not enough to help you let go of them altogether. That's why you need to learn to reprogram yourself.

As a child, you had little control over your circumstances. But as an adult, you have the responsibility, choice and power to undo this negative programming and free yourself to experience the happiness, success, health and wealth you desire and deserve.

Self-awareness around the past and present is key to transforming your negative, self-limiting beliefs.

 Reprogramming Your Beliefs in Seven Steps

1. Whenever you face a challenge in achieving something that, on paper, looks like something you should be able to do, focus on the thoughts and feelings you experience when considering the challenge and working toward it. Write them down—often, they'll be self-defeating statements you've heard in your head for so long, you don't realize they're untrue.

2. Write down any other repetitive internal dialogue you have with yourself. This includes your internal monologue, or "monkey mind chatter."

3. Look at the notes you've taken from steps one and two and identify the common strings of thought that represent your self-limiting beliefs.

4. Write down where you think these beliefs came from, what situations brought them on, which people introduced them, and why they came about. What was your take on these situations and the resulting beliefs that formed in you?

5. Take each self-limiting belief and challenge it by asking these questions:

- Is this true?

- If not, why? (Think about all the verifiable things you've done that debunk this self-limiting belief.)

- Are my thoughts regarding this rational or irrational, factual or false?

- Why?

- Is there another way of looking at this statement? Should it be reinterpreted into something positive?

6. If you could rewrite these beliefs into their positive version, what would they say? Rewrite and rephrase each belief into a positive.

7. Repeat these reframed positive beliefs aloud to yourself each day. Eventually, you'll start to believe them.

Low Self-Esteem and Self-Image

 Self-limiting, negative beliefs lead to low self-esteem and a poor self-image. This negativity clings to us, like a foul aura, and casts its harmful, depressing shadow over all our life experiences. It hurts our chances before we even start going after a goal.

Some of the messages you need to be concerned about include thoughts and beliefs such as:

- You can't do that.

- NO!

- DON'T!

- You're not good enough.

68

- You can't achieve that.

- You're not capable.

- You're just going to fail and fall flat on your face.

Here's the good news: these messages have power only if we haven't taken action to change them. It takes a very determined, persistent, self-aware person to come to understand their subconscious mind, but it IS possible to.

In my book, *Designing Your Life*, I discuss the intricacies of the subconscious and conscious minds and ways to help control them in order to create the life you've always dreamed of. For this book, I'll keep the example short and sweet. Our subconscious motivation is to keep us safe. So, when we set our sights on a goal chosen with our conscious mind—one that may stretch beyond our comfort zone—our subconscious, with very pure intentions, will work to make sure we stay safe, comfortable and unhurt.

For example, you may set a new goal and start taking action toward achieving it, but then lose interest along the way. Perhaps you start to become unsure whether you really want it, or doubt whether you're prepared to do the work, or you feel discomfort about having your time compromised by more requests and demands. So, your new goal loses steam or just doesn't work out as you had originally envisioned. You feel bad. You don't understand why you can't or didn't achieve what you thought you wanted. You see others around you who seem to achieve their goals so easily and your self-esteem and self-image are impacted. Then, you feel down and dejected and don't completely understand what went wrong.

Self-Esteem Reprogramming in 10 Steps

1. Identify your areas of low or easily undermined self-esteem and self-image. Write these down.

2. Identify how these shortfalls formed. What early childhood incidents do you think gave rise to these feelings? What later life experiences may also have contributed?

3. Identify the triggers that ignite your feelings of low self-esteem and self-image. For example, being criticized or bullied, having an argument, feeling that others disapprove of you, a work challenge, personal crisis at home, etc.

4. What are your thoughts, emotions and beliefs surrounding these issues? Identify those that are negative and those that are positive.

5. Ask the following questions to challenge each of your low self-esteem thoughts:

- Is this true?

- If not, why? (Back up with hard data when possible.)

71

- Are my thoughts regarding this rational or irrational, factual or false?

- Why?

- Is there another way of looking at this statement? Should it be reinterpreted into something positive?

6. Make a proactive choice and effort to focus on the positive. Always try to look on the bright side. Remember there's always a positive angle. Everything in life revolves around your perceptions of situations, and you can choose to have positive perceptions rather than negative ones.

7. Be kind to yourself.

Kindness begins with gratitude, so think about the good things you already have. Remind yourself of things that have gone well, either in the past or recently. Consider the skills you've used to cope with challenging situations.

Then, move on to forgiveness. Forgive yourself and others who have hurt you. Don't be so hard on yourself. Don't jump to negative conclusions.

The final act of kindness revolves around healing yourself. Access your inner higher self and ask what you need to do to heal these feelings, hurts and self-esteem issues.

Understanding Negative Self-Worth

While self-esteem dictates how confident you are, self-worth determines the value you place on yourself, your opinion and your time. Many people have issues assessing their self-worth. Without being able to accurately gauge their value, they allow themselves to be undervalued and abused by others. This works to worsen their self-esteem and self-worth, which starts the cycle over and over.

The challenge here is to overcome those feelings of low self-worth and build up the inner interpretation of your value. The first step in doing so is to develop your self-awareness. After all, if you know yourself—if you're aware of your strengths and your legitimate weaknesses—you'll be far less likely to accept someone else's description of you. You can do this by applying the self-esteem exercises in Chapter 3 to your various issues of self-worth.

Poverty Consciousness

 Poverty consciousness is another issue often developed in childhood. We are very receptive to absorbing the messages we pick up from adults. If your parents had financial struggles while you were growing up and frequently argued about money, your subconscious likely associates money with conflict and disagreement, so you unknowingly push it away from you. This makes sense on an instinctual level—why wouldn't you push away unpleasant, uncomfortable things? But you have to override this instinct and reprogram it because it's not actually being helpful.

Likewise, upon asking for something as a child, you may have been told that money doesn't grow on trees. You may have come away from that experience believing deep down that there just is not enough to go around, ever. After all, if your parents—two adults you trusted and idolized—couldn't get enough money, how could you possibly dream of doing so? A part of you may even feel as if you're betraying your parents if you're more financially successful than they are. All of this is pure bunk that you've got to learn to let go of.

Of course, not every negative thought surrounding money is about its limited availability. Maybe your parents took a different approach, teaching you that rich people were greedy and bad, so your subconscious associates money with being bad, underhanded and deceptive. Or maybe they believed, and as a result, taught you, that money isn't spiritual. Many people in healing professions carry this belief, finding it hard to ask for money according to their value and worth; therefore, their practices or businesses struggle and suffer.

On the positive side, your experience is not unique. You'd be amazed to discover how many people out there hold onto these same subconscious limits and resentments toward money. And I was one of them. In my childhood, I remember hearing a lot about money not growing on trees. This implied to me that money was a limited resource that I should never expect to have in abundance. This deeply affected my concept of what was possible in terms of income and assets. Luckily, once I saw the effect that this subconscious understanding had on me, I was able to overcome it. In doing so, and by finding financial success, I've discovered all of these situations to be littered with untruths, misunderstandings and biases that damage each of us. In a way, it's like holding onto the belief that if you step on a crack, your mother's back will suddenly and mysteriously break. It somehow makes sense to you as a child—but as an adult, you can see through that faulty reasoning.

Likewise, you can cut through poverty consciousness and develop prosperity consciousness. This understanding of the shift between poverty consciousness and prosperity was what led me to write *You Deserve to Be Rich*, a book that explores this concept in far more depth than I have here.

From Poverty Consciousness to Prosperity Consciousness

You can shift and transform your poverty consciousness to a prosperity consciousness once you learn the secret to accessing and reprogramming your subconscious beliefs.

Poverty Consciousness Reprogramming in Seven Steps

1. Identify your negative thoughts about money and write them down.

2. Identify how these feelings formed and from what experiences. What early childhood incidents could have contributed to these feelings? What later life experiences may also have contributed?

3. Identify the triggers that ignite your feelings of poverty consciousness. For example, getting a raise at work, receiving a bonus, getting a tax return, etc.

4. What are your thoughts, emotions and beliefs surrounding these issues? For example, when you receive a large sum of money, do you feel guilty, uncomfortable or unworthy and give it away? Do you spend it quickly, as if keeping it will hurt you in some way? Write down your interpretation of what these situations mean.

5. Apply the questioning technique to challenge each of your poverty consciousness thoughts:

- Is this true?

- If not, why? (Back up with hard data when possible.)

- Are my thoughts regarding this rational or irrational, factual or false?

- Why?

- Is there another way of looking at this statement? Should it be reinterpreted into something positive?

6. Choose to focus on the positive. Always try to look on the bright side. Remember there is always a positive angle— everything is about perception and how you choose to look at a situation. When you get that large sum of money that initially makes you feel uncomfortable, push those impulses away and think of all the reasons you are grateful to have it. Think of all the good things you can do for yourself and others when you have financial stability and success.

7. Be forgiving. Forgive yourself and others who have hurt you financially, because hanging onto that resentment will do nothing but keep you mired in financial difficulties. Here's the thing: I know this is a lot easier said than done. I know how it feels to be betrayed and how hard it is to forgive when the feelings are still fresh. But by holding on to the resentment, you

aren't hurting the person who betrayed you—you're hurting yourself. Give yourself the relief and space to heal by letting go. Further, don't be so hard on yourself. Don't jump to negative conclusions. Next, access your inner higher self and ask what you need to do to heal these feelings.

Fears: Good versus Bad

———•●•———

"Fear only exists when you do not understand that you have the power to project thought and that the Universe will respond."

— Esther Hicks

"Make failure your teacher, not your undertaker."

— Zig Ziglar

"Fear feeds failure; desire feeds your destiny."
— Jill Koenig

———•●•———

 There are many forms of fear you can feel from day to day. Fear of failure and, conversely, fear of success are prime examples of the vast range that fear can take. Both can be debilitating, keeping you stuck— for completely opposite reasons.

Likewise, there are good fears and bad fears. Have you considered the difference between the two types of fear?

In its natural, pure state, fear is a form of self-protection, which makes it easy to understand how it can be good. You learn that fire is hot, so the fear you feel when fire is large and coming at you saves your life. Good fear can be your ally. At some point in human evolution, bad fear began surfacing, fear that wasn't objectively correct or predictive of danger, but instead rose from our feelings and perceptions—extremely biased and unreliable judges. Bad fear can be a devastating, counterproductive enemy and should be squashed if you want to succeed.

Learning to recognize which type of fear you're responding to is critical to your success.

Bad Fear

Bad fear doesn't move you forward, it paralyzes you; it keeps you from doing the things you need to do to succeed.

Bad fear also keeps you from taking responsibility, because it's based on incorrect perceptions. Perceptions are the driver of decisions, actions and results.

Finally, bad fear stresses and frightens you.

Good Fear

Good fear is the result of accurate perception and taking responsibility for yourself. You know what you should be doing when you're responding to good fear. Good fear also:

- Keeps you vigilant.

- Gets you out of bed in the morning.

- Forces you to confront your bad fears, limiting beliefs and bad habits.

Harness your good fears because they help you sharpen your edge. They also help shake you out of your comfort zone and move you forward to try new things. Good fears motivate you to take risks to see what you can achieve.

Fear of Failure versus Fear of Success

The fear of failure and the fear of success are both paralyzing emotions. These fears lurk deep within, like dreaded monsters and ghouls who hide and take up residence inside your head, unbeknownst to you.

At first you may think these two fears are one in the same, but that couldn't be further from the truth. They do have many of the same symptoms; both hold you back from achieving your dreams and goals. But, there are key differences.

Fear of Failure

The fear of failure freezes you, often preventing you from even getting started toward a goal. This fear reveals itself through extreme, unattainable perfectionism or an extreme aversion to criticism.

Fear of Success

The fear of success is a far more confusing, complicated fear. It's also difficult to understand because it's principally based in your subconscious. It's like an unpredictable, shifty chameleon and is more common than you may think.

The fear of success works like this. You'll start out making good progress, achieving your goals and aspirations. You'll know what you want and take action to get it. Once you start making progress and, even in the early days, can see the reality of eventual success—BAM!—fear of success rears its ugly, monstrous head and sabotages your every effort.

Does that sound familiar? If it's not something you do, I bet you know someone who does. I remember working with one agent who was generally on-point. They did great work and had a vast amount of knowledge, but every time they were about to take a huge step forward in their business they would suddenly start slacking off, miss work and have family issues that weren't legitimate. All because they were afraid to succeed!

Digging deep to find the reasons behind your fear takes a heightened sense of self-awareness as well as a commitment to self-analysis and understanding.

Fear of success may hide itself in the following feelings, actions and thoughts (in no particular order):

- **Feeling concerned over losing freedom, anonymity and safety.** Common statements and thoughts that illustrate this include:

  "I don't want to lose my freedom and time when things get busier. Yes, I want success, but I don't want to have to put myself out there in open view and become more public about my work."

  "I'm concerned about compromising myself with longer working hours, added responsibilities, workloads that grow too much, and clients who take up too much of my time. I don't want to have to do presentations and deliver speeches and be so responsible for other people. It's best I stay safe and in control of myself, my time and my freedom."

- **Feeling undeserving.** Underneath, you may feel that you don't deserve to have success in your life. Subconsciously, you self-sabotage your relationships, work, business activities, plans and dreams by struggling with and convincing yourself that you're not good enough to achieve them.

You don't speak proudly about your achievements and are unable to accept compliments graciously. You downplay your accomplishments and prefer to be coy and shy away from the limelight for those few seconds.

- **Procrastination.** You avoid taking action that moves you forward. Time goes by and you sabotage and derail your project or goal. More missed and lost opportunities pile up.

- **Fearing what success will bring.** You are scared of all the consequences of success, including the need to work harder, longer hours, exhaustion and compromised time with family. You also dread facing the sense of entitlement from family and friends asking for favors, demanding or implying that you should help them by giving them money. You fear that people will turn against you through jealousy and/or that you'll develop new enemies in the workplace.

- **Guilt about your success because others aren't experiencing it.** "I want to achieve my goals, but doing so might make my friends or family feel inadequate."

- **Fear of being harshly judged.** You fear being judged harshly and criticized, with cynicism, jealousy and rejection by your circle of family, friends and associates if you achieve too much. You worry that people will think you're a know-it-all or an egotist.

Eradicating Fear of Failure and Success in Seven Steps

The more you identify your fears and fight to bring them to the surface to analyze and challenge them, the more likely you are to defuse and disable them.

You can significantly reduce your resistance and reluctance to achieve your goals if you stack yourself for success. Focus on succeeding in spite of the odds. At the end of the day, it's a clear choice between playing small and hiding behind the anonymity of living a quiet, safe, underachieving life or stepping up to play big, putting yourself out there and living up to your fullest potential.

1. Get very clear on any subconscious beliefs that may relate to your fear of failure and success. Write down these beliefs and what you think about them when you hold them up to the cold light of day.

2. Note your observations and what you've learned about your particular fears and how they manifest themselves.

3. For each fear of failure you've identified, make note of any upsides/positives and downsides/negatives.

4. Give each manifestation a rating on a scale of 0-10 (with 0 being low/not scary, and 10 being high/very scary).

Repeat steps one through four for your fears of success.

5. Visualize an ideal outcome for the time when you've achieved the goal you desire. Now, write down which of your success and failure fears could legitimately happen within that scenario, and how you can positively deal with them.

6. As you achieve small wins, write them down in your Victory Journal.

7. Always try to maintain a positive mindset. If you find yourself slipping into negative thinking patterns, switch yourself using the techniques discussed in Chapter 4.

Turning Failure Experiences into Successes

You may have failed many times throughout your life, but those individual failings don't make YOU a failure. You learn from your mistakes and you will rise again, wiser from the experience.

Believe it or not, successful people actually welcome failure. They see the failure experience as bringing them a step closer to achieving success—like a debugging, refining process so that, by the next try, they've eliminated (or significantly reduced) the chance of failure and vastly increased their probability of success.

Let's have a look at what some successful people have said about failure. Their words are both informative and inspiring.

"Success consists of going from failure to failure without loss of enthusiasm."

— Winston Churchill

"It is fine to celebrate success, but it is more important to heed the lessons of failure."

— Bill Gates

"I can accept failure; everyone fails at something. But I can't accept not trying."

— Michael Jordan

"Every adversity, every failure, every heartache carries with it the seed on an equal or greater benefit."

— Napoleon Hill

"The price of Success is much lower than the price of Failure."

— Zig Ziglar

"Far better is it to dare mighty things, to win glorious triumphs, even though checkered by failure ... than to rank with those poor

spirits who neither enjoy nor suffer much, because they live in a gray twilight that knows not victory nor defeat."

— Theodore Roosevelt

"A man can fail many times, but he isn't a failure until he begins to blame somebody else."

— John Burroughs

"Before success comes in any man's life, he's sure to meet with much temporary defeat and, perhaps some failures. When defeat overtakes a man, the easiest and the most logical thing to do is to quit. That's exactly what the majority of men do."

— Napoleon Hill

 Turning Failures into Success in Seven Steps

1. Write down your most recent failure.

2. Record what you understand about the facts surrounding that failure.

3. Make a note of how this will affect future decisions you make.

4. What are some ways that failure may actually help you find success?

5. Research some successful people who've experienced the same or similar failure and who persevered in spite of that (or, maybe, because of it).

6. After reading and absorbing this section on fear and failure, what have you learned about failure and its lessons?

7. How will you look at your future failures as they occur?

Conquering Feeling Overwhelmed

"Annihilate 'overwhelm' thinking. It's simply a symptom."

— Jeanna Gabellini

 Life really is simple, but we insist on making it more complicated than it should be. It's almost as if we're afraid of its simplicity—like we're missing out if we allow it to be uncomplicated. Often, our inner voices in their negativity chorus say things like, "Oh, I'm so overwhelmed" or, "I've got information overload and I just don't know what to do about it, or which way to turn."

More often than not, however, that's an illusion or excuse. In fact, what you're really dealing with is a bad case of indecision.

Yes, for sure, information is coming at us from all directions. On average, a person today receives more information daily than their counterpart received in an entire lifetime 100 years ago. However, while most of the information received by the person 100 years ago was vital to life, the information we get today is mostly noise—chatter to fill our minds and snag our attention. At the end of the day, the information you decide to actually take in is a matter of choice. It's your choice to control your mind and to filter the content you allow in, leaving out anything that isn't essential to your life.

I know people who read just about every email that comes into their inbox, and that is seriously ridiculous. Honestly—that is a wasteful, time-consuming distraction that's often the result of a desire to avoid the things that really matter and need to be dealt with. In other words, it's a delay tactic. You're probably guilty of it too. How often do you check your Facebook, Twitter, email or favorite blogs before taking on some task you're dreading? My guess is, often.

Controlling the content that goes into your head isn't just about filtering out the noise, however. It's also about understanding the reason you're trying to be indecisive. Most people are indecisive because they're afraid to make a wrong decision. It's natural to want to avoid making a mistake and to want things to work out perfectly, whether it's a personal or professional issue.

But perfection is often found in the most imperfect ways. The perfect journey is one that includes lots of lessons—lessons that are usually found when making mistakes. Thus, the perfect journey includes many missteps. No one knows this better than BP Capital Management hedge fund Founder T. Boone Pickens who, as a teen, entered into a deal with his grandmother to mow the lawns of her rental homes for a summer. Because he didn't pay attention to the details, he ended up getting paid far too little to do way more work than he expected. That's just one example of how a successful person benefited from making a mistake—there are thousands of others. Can you feel your shoulders releasing some of their stress? Just knowing that your most perfect journey actually MUST include mistakes is such a relief! It changes your focus completely from trying to avoid mistakes to enjoying the process and being positive along the way.

Some people try to protect themselves from failure, but the irony is that they're really pushing success further away. As mentioned before, we all know people who seem to achieve what they want more easily and make their goals happen and manifest much faster than we seem to be able to. You've probably spent a good amount of time wondering why and how they do it—what's in their magic success formula?

Some people follow specified steps, like a recipe, to a T and don't complicate the process with the usual overanalytical head stuff. They set aside their ego and don't agonize. They refuse to trap themselves in a mental wrestling match that inevitably leads to feeling overwhelmed: what **to** do, what **not** to do, which one to do first, which to save for last and when to do it all. They simplify and get on with the job.

They recognize that prior success leaves a trail of breadcrumbs, so why reinvent the wheel? Just follow those crumbs and do what other successful people have done.

"Model someone who's already successful, because success leaves clues."

— Tony Robbins

"If you want to achieve success, all you need to do is find a way to model those who have already succeeded."

— Tony Robbins

————————•◆•————————

If you've been planning to reach a certain goal, chances are good that you instinctively know all the right steps to take already. Maybe you've been questioning your instincts, thinking that it should be that easy or that you must have missed something. But the truth is that your subconscious has already worked your path out to the best of its ability and now all that's left to do is get started. Follow each step, stop overthinking it and don't question yourself. It really is that simple.

Most people are talkers; few people are doers. Feelings of being overwhelmed and overloaded are merely excuses to continue being a talker and avoiding the unknown world of doers.

With that said, it's important to note that there might be times you legitimately get stuck. If you really aren't sure what next steps you should take, and you aren't suffering from being overwhelmed as a result of too much useless information, reach out and ask for help. There's absolutely nothing wrong with that. In Chapter 6, I'll help you learn how to build relationships that support and bolster you, which is exactly what you want when you need help.

We can't always do it all on our own. In fact, it's a lot better to collaborate with others, pooling your combined strengths, skills and talents. When you ask someone for help, ask questions, listen intently and then act. Take decisive action steps immediately. With consistent application, you're likely to reach your desired destination.

In my personal and professional experience, I've come across inspired, creative people with great talent and potential who are committed and willing to do the work. They're not lazy or lacking motivation. They simply feel stuck and unsure about where to start or how to do what needs to be done to achieve their dreams and goals. This causes a paralyzing effect that quickly overtakes them and squashes their hopes.

It's almost as though they slip into a trancelike state when looking at the plethora of things to be done. But instead of actually doing any of them, they waste time questioning themselves over and over, never allowing their journey to start.

It doesn't have to be that way. The real shame is that it's actually easy to break out of this funk. In fact, it can be done in just seven steps.

Breaking Free of That Overwhelmed Feeling in Seven Steps

Are you ready to get unstuck and start achieving amazing results? Here's what I've found works. You can try each of these tips all at once or implement just one action step per day.

1. Force yourself to keep it simple. Make that your key aim. Don't look at every possible scenario, every potential outcome or every noticeable caveat. Focus on your goals and tasks in broad strokes. It really does take the angst out of the situation.

2. Keep alert and do not allow indecision to take over.

3. Focus on implementing one new action per day. For example, when participating in a training call or webinar, or doing a home-study program, take one key step or key gem to implement each day, rather than feeling completely overwhelmed because you have to do everything all at once.

By doing a little bit each day, the right habits will eventually become ingrained. You'll begin thinking more positively and develop higher self-esteem, both of which will help you tackle whatever you may have going on in your life.

4. Record your victories in your Victory Journal. The aim is to fully experience the joy and accomplishment of taking small steps forward so that you're inspired to create even more wins as your confidence, optimism, power and strength increase.

5. Highlight your fears. If they're distracting you from simplifying and making you indecisive, uncover them and face them. Often, just saying out loud what you're afraid of will take the power out of the fear completely.

6. Choose one fear and write down five ways to overcome it. As you do, you'll show yourself how silly the fear is and that knowledge will make all your fears less dominant.

7. Limit your information. If you generally read every email each day, or look at a dozen blogs and news sources, plus mine your Twitter and Facebook feeds, then you may be overstimulated with junk information. Wean yourself down to just one or two news sources (make exceptions when you're actively researching); read one or two social networks once per day.

Chapter 4:
Exploring Optimism

One of the most powerful allies you can have is optimism. Optimism is like a secret knife hidden in your boot that cuts through negativity, stunts defeatism and immobilizes self-hatred. Before 1829, there was no entry for optimism's opposite—pessimism—in Webster's dictionary. I wonder how much it would have benefited everyone if it'd never been added, and optimism was our only option?

What Is Optimism?

 Optimism is the attitude that anything is possible, that the future has no boundaries. It's a winning combination of hopefulness and confidence that carries you forward through the most difficult times.

Optimism isn't something that you get from the outside; it's something that grows from the inside out. It starts deep inside your stomach, a kernel of hope and confidence that no matter what the world looks like now, your future is bright and assured.

Optimism is like an animal. It's hungry and it looks for things to feed it. Negativity is like a poison apple, so optimism avoids it entirely. Instead, optimism feeds on positive things, people, energy and events. And the more you feed it these things, the bigger, stronger and more powerful it gets.

How It Affects the Positive Edge

Do you want to know the most important thing about optimism? It knows more than you do. Optimism is a feeling that requires you to be confident about a limit-free future. But optimism isn't a fantasy, so how can that be?

Here's an exercise that will help. Think of everything you know as sitting inside a box. This would include the days you've already experienced, the moments you're going through right this very minute and all your memories. These things all fit inside a box that optimism does not fit in. Because optimism doesn't work on the past or present, it works on the future. It's too big for your box, so it rests outside the box where it can see all these amazing things that aren't yet but eventually will be in the box. You can't see these things now, but you will once you've experienced them and they're in your box. From this we get the saying, "Hindsight is 20/20."

Do you remember the old game show "Let's Make a Deal"? In that show, the host would offer people prizes, some of which could not be seen because they were behind a door. Your optimism already knows what's behind all the closed doors in your future. Not only that, but optimism knows just how exciting those things are. By allowing yourself to fully feel optimism, you kick-start the positive edge snowball and help ensure that the future you attract is a positive one.

Tipping the Scales for Optimism

After a lifetime of negativity, fear and doubt, it's difficult to buy into the concept of optimism—I can completely understand that. Let me share with you the way that I changed my own thinking and went from being apprehensive about the future to allowing optimism to stake its claim.

Instead of letting go of my negativity or apprehension completely, I decided instead to simply tip the scales. Instead of being over 50 percent fearful of the future and less than 50 percent optimistic, I had to do whatever it took to become at least 51 percent optimistic and 49 percent apprehensive in order to get the positive momentum rolling. On the surface, that meant reversing as little as 2 percent of my negativity. That doesn't sound hard or scary, does it? Yet that 2 percent was enough to completely change the future and opportunities that I attracted to myself.

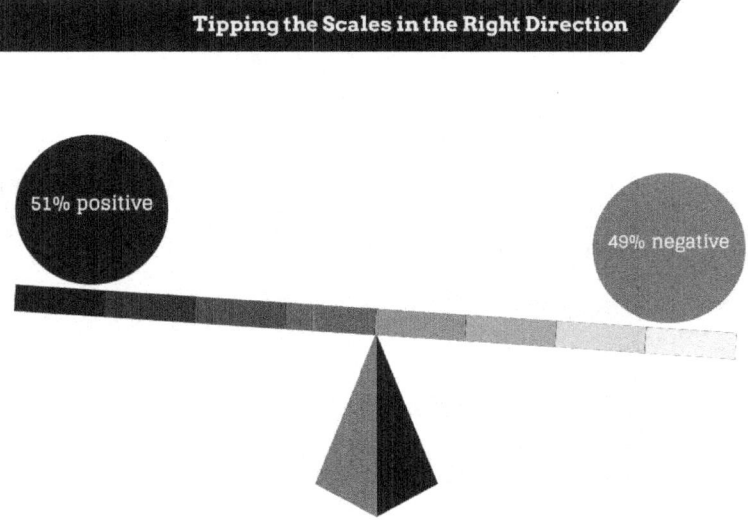

In the end, you have to do whatever it takes to tip the scale. Until you get this right, it just doesn't make sense to move forward because you will get knocked back again and again until you figure it out. Mentally change the mountain of obstacles in front of you into a tiny hill, and then set out on your journey.

The positive edge isn't about becoming a zombie who smiles all the time and refuses to think critically about the realities of life. The positive edge is about filling your thoughts and perceptions with a majority of positivity, joy and optimism and pushing negativity into the minority. It's about understanding that bad things happen and negativity can be based on real-world events, but also knowing that there is hope, there are solutions, and that you're willing and able to find them.

It only takes a 2 percent shift to allow positivity to win and exert its amazing influence over your life. Can you spare that 2 percent? Or, a better question, can you afford *not* to?

You have to permit yourself to receive all the good that life has to offer. By scaling back slightly on your negativity so that positivity is the winner, even by a very small margin, you show yourself and the universe that you are choosing happiness, optimism and joy rather than anger, fear and resentment, that you are open to receiving gifts—and you won't return them to sender.

Your Perceptions Influence the Way You See the World

Your perceptions—the way your senses and brain interpret stimulus—have a very powerful influence on the way you see and experience the world.

Two people can perceive the same situation in very different ways, depending on mindset, inner emotional filters, life experiences and their tendency to be positive, negative or somewhere in between.

While it may sound like an automated process, your own perception (which is what everything really boils down to) is actually a choice. You can choose how you ultimately look at a situation or experience.

Think about a time when you've been in a really bad mood or watched someone else who was, and how nothing went right. Even more obstacles and negative experiences popped up along the pathway and seemed to escalate in direct correlation to the person's worsening mood.

Things went from bad to worse. You (or the other person) felt down and hopeless, as if the situation would never get better. That's what happens when an individual is operating at a low-energy vibration level. It is this vibration that determines their experience and how they interpret what is happening.

Now, think about a time when you (or someone else) were in a really good mood and operating at a high-energy vibration. Everything flowed easily and naturally; positive events and outcomes slotted nicely into place. It was as though you (or the other individual) had the magic touch, creating win-wins for everyone concerned, which made you feel even happier, more satisfied and fulfilled.

We've all known at least one person for which everything comes easy. That person isn't blessed by some outside energy nor are they better or more deserving than you. They just know, often intuitively, how to ride that high-energy vibration and avoid falling off. Now, it's your turn to hitch a ride and gain the positive edge.

Positivity Renovation in Seven Steps

1. Set aside some time today to look at a situation or person you're not happy with and flip it around to consider from a more positive perspective. Can you see the situation or person from a different point of view? What positives can you see in this from the perspective of a learning experience?

2. Try this in reverse also. Take a positive situation and flip it around to view from a negative perspective. Write down your observations. Can you see how fluid this can be, how you can easily think of everything this way? Make sure you flip your view of the situation back around to a positive one before you finish with this exercise.

3. What are some situations you've been viewing negatively that have created a domino effect of misery and interruption from your goal?

4. How can you turn each of these situations around in order to see them more positively?

5. What past actions would you have done differently if you'd seen these situations as positives?

6. What actions can you take now as a result of converting them from negative to positive?

7. Always remember that it is within your power to decide how you choose to look at your experiences with people and events in your life.

Optimism Underscoring Action

In the beginning of this chapter, I explained how optimism is an attitude that anything is possible. You may be wondering how positivity is different from optimism. Positivity is the underlying belief that everything is good, that bad things happen for good reasons and that any situation can be reframed in a way that benefits you.

But optimism is even more forceful than this. While you must have positivity in order to create a positive edge, if you can combine it with optimism—that undefeatable belief that anything is possible—you'll find your success increasing exponentially. It's the difference between seeing a closed door in front of you and saying, "Whatever's behind that door, it's for the best," and, "Whatever's behind that door is going to be amazing."

Chapter 5:

Your Success and Happiness Mindset

By now, if you've applied the lessons taught in this book, you've started experiencing forward motion in your positivity. You feel better, stand taller and have much more hope for the future. But if you want this snowball to turn into a snowboulder, you have to go further; you have to **start taking action.**

Knowledge is only powerful when you actually apply it to your life. In order to achieve success and happiness in both my personal and business lives, I had to learn to put into action all these same lessons I'm giving you. And to continue furthering the success and happiness, I make it a point to see the good in the world and to stay in a positive mindset. Which is a pretty fun action to take, if you think about it.

I'm going to be completely honest with you: there are days when this can be a big challenge. So much of the news we're exposed to daily is fraught with problems, fear, scarcity and violence that some days, it takes a concerted effort to remain positive.

The work I put into this—and that I suggest you put into it—doesn't go to waste, though. In fact, it helps to make those dark days more bearable, almost serving to redeem them completely. Our mindset and attitude will determine how well we succeed in achieving our goals and how well we bounce back when faced with a challenge. We are not victims to a predetermined mindset; we control it. And that means you can call that power up at any time and completely reverse the course of your day, week or month. You have that amazing power—so use it.

Life responds to your attitude, whether positive or negative. But life doesn't *just* respond—it responds in kind. Do you want life to send a response filled with positivity or one filled with negativity? I think we both know the answer to that question.

Success and Happiness Mindset

 How much would you like to be able to instantly acquire the attitude of a winner? It's not as hard as you think. First, let's understand why it's so necessary. If you want to live a fulfilling, successful and productive life, you must learn to cultivate a happiness mindset.

This mindset is your responsibility to develop. There's no one in your life who's been officially appointed to make you happy. You must figure out how to make yourself happy. If you look outward for it, you'll absolutely never find it. It'd be like trying to see your soul reflected in someone else's eyes.

 Embracing the Success and Happiness Mindset Shift in Seven Steps

1. Make a commitment to switch your thinking to the positive. Every time you catch yourself thinking negatively about

something or someone, immediately pull back and switch to a positive alternative. For example, if your mind starts throwing thoughts out such as, "I'm so bad at this," immediately replace it with a new thought, such as, "I'm so much better at this now, and I'm going to keep getting better!"

2. When you're having trouble getting into a positive frame of mind, remember positive experiences in the past that made you feel really happy. These can trigger your ability to switch to a positive outlook.

I recommend that you spend some time selecting these experiences ahead of time so that you have them ready to go when needed. You could also use a physical signifier or stimulus, like clicking your fingers or a clap of your hands, to snap yourself out of the negative-thought loop and prompt the switch to positive thoughts.

You might also try selecting positive sayings and words that have meaning to you personally and represent what you most want. Repeat them out loud several times each day, and make sure you say them with energy. Whatever sayings you choose, make certain they are things that you believe with all your heart.

Attitude is not simply a state of mind. It's also a reflection of your values, emotions, heart and spirit. Your attitude is defined by more than just *saying*, "I can do it." It's defined by actually *believing* you can.

Here are some positive, empowering affirmations to help get you started.

- "I can do it!"

- "I believe in myself."

- "I am going to do this right now and enjoy my win thoroughly."

- "If I believe it, I can see it, and then achieve it."

- "I am reaching my goals perfectly, in a synchronistic way, every day. Serendipity is my ally."

- "I can overcome any hurdle, obstacle or curveball that comes my way."

- "I am getting stronger and more determined every single day."

- "From every setback, I learn great lessons that help me tweak my plan for progress and ultimate success."

- "Every day I am getting closer and closer to realizing my goals in life."

- "With the progress of each day, my attitude is becoming more positive and resilient, and I bounce back faster."

3. Write your affirmation somewhere you're likely to see it several times a day. The more you repeat your trigger sayings and words, the greater their effect will be on your attitude and the quicker they'll become part of your daily process.

4. Avoid negative people who only have disparaging things to say. You know the ones—people who can only make negative remarks about events and people, the ones who wipe a smile off your face within 10 minutes of being together. Sometimes you have to move them out of your life, either temporarily or permanently.

5. Don't watch the news for seven days. During this experiment, notice the difference in your overall mood and outlook. Continue to do this at regular intervals on an ongoing basis. Think of it as an information fast.

The media focuses primarily on negative news stories. That's their bread and butter. But there's not much you can do about the bad news that batters your brain each day, so it's best to avoid it. If you're concerned that this will leave you too uninvolved, set up a regular donation to an organization such as the Red Cross so that you're already helping out when the next disaster hits. You can also pay attention to the news leading up to any voting deadlines so that you understand the issues at play and can make informed decisions at the ballot.

6. First thing in the morning before you get out of bed, listen to inspirational and motivational audios. This is a great way to start your day while you're in the very receptive alpha phase, a time when you're very open to suggestion.

This is also a good time to listen to audio programs with techniques and practices that help you reduce or eliminate anxiety, fear, worry, lethargy and lack of motivation from your life so that you can make positive changes and raise your energy vibration level.

7. Subscribe to an email service or download an app that delivers daily inspirational quotes, thought-provoking messages or positive news stories to you. Some messages may be funny while others will bring meaningful tears to your eyes. You could also receive messages via inspirational videos. No matter how you receive the positive message, by taking it in, you become part of a positivity chain that spreads positive energy out into the world.

Remember to write down in your Victory Journal any observations about the effects of each of these steps as well as the victories they bring.

The Power of Positive Thinking

 Positivity is undoubtedly the most important factor of success, so it's a really good thing that positive thinking is a choice. When you consider the fact that positive thinking brings positive results while negative thinking brings on negative consequences, the attitude choice you must make is obvious.

Even if you forget about like attracting like, positive thinking just plain feels good. When we think positively, we feel optimistic, hopeful, happy and energized because our bodies release chemicals such as serotonin, which give us good vibes and a sense of well-being.

We're not all wired to be positive by nature. Some people are more naturally disposed to negativity, spending much of their time and energy in the pit of negative doldrums. Instead of seeing their cup half full, they see it as half empty. But it doesn't have to be this way. If you're one of the negative-by-nature folks, don't worry—you can choose to be a positive person. And you can do so successfully. Just by picking up this book, you've proven that there's a seed of optimism inside you. Now it's time to water it and help it grow.

No matter where you find yourself on the sliding scale of positive to negative, it's up to you to choose which way you **want** to go. The person you end up being will depend entirely on the mindset you've chosen.

Choosing positivity will lead you to a happier, healthier, more successful and fulfilled life. It will deeply influence the aspects of life that mean the most to you, including relationships, wellness, career and wealth.

It's just like the law of attraction and quantum physics tells us: what we think about most is what we experience and become. That's a compelling reason to work on your positive mindset and spend as much time as possible being optimistic.

According to Deepak Chopra, best-selling author and MD, our brains produce chemicals called neuropeptides, which are molecules of emotion such as fear, joy and love. They're not only present in our brain but also flow throughout our entire body. Neuropeptide chemicals can, when directed to, promote feelings of self-assurance, influence and power. As these neuropeptides circulate throughout your body, they have a huge impact on your immune system. If you envision yourself as a healthy person who cannot get sick, your immune system cells reinforce themselves to make sure that you have the ability to fight off illnesses and disease.

These cells of emotion are intelligent, thinking cells, always listening in on the conversation you're having with yourself. They pay attention to both your conscious and subconscious self-talk and, accordingly, they adapt their response based on what they hear you saying and thinking.

It follows that, from a scientific viewpoint, you already potentially possess within you the power to change your life; you just need to spend most of your time thinking powerful, positive thoughts pointed in the right direction. In fact, you won't just change your external response to situations, thus creating positive change, you'll actually change your physical self and influence your overall health and well-being.

Just imagine what would happen if you started thinking powerful, positive thoughts more regularly—how much better you'd feel, how much happier your life would be. It's not difficult—all you have to do is actively incorporate happy, powerful, hopeful thoughts. Here are a few to get you started:

- "I am powerful and can achieve anything I set my mind to!"

- "I have strength and endurance beyond my wildest expectations!"

- "Nothing can stop me!"

- "I can easily overcome the challenges I face each day."

- "I can't wait to see how I progress on my journey today."

- "I can't wait to see what challenges are waiting for me and how I can conquer them!"

Further help your thinking cells by thinking about a powerful, confident person you admire. One who embodies the confidence you wish to emulate. Or envision an idealized, powerfully confident image of yourself. If your ideal person or image is fearless, your cells of emotion relating to fear will create more neuropeptide chemicals that promote feelings of fearlessness and overall well-being.

Positive, optimistic people win and do better overall, often in surprising, amazing ways. Their bodies are programmed to make sure of that.

Feel Better about Yourself Instantly!

We all have down days when our self-esteem is low, we have the blues or we just don't feel as chipper as usual. Perhaps something happened to make you feel down, or you don't feel like you have the energy to make the effort that day. Seasonally, it's quite common in colder months to have the winter blues and a general sense of cabin fever due to limited mobility and the early nights.

Those early winter sunsets can also have a physiological effect as we lose some of our ability to produce vitamin D, a vitamin that aids in the absorption of calcium and phosphorous for healthy bones and muscles. There is also a strong link between a lack of vitamin D and feelings of depression, laziness and sadness as the vitamin works on the part of your brain linked to depression. When we feel down, it can affect just about every area of our lives—from our health and well-being to our relationships with family and friends. It also affects our ability to get along with others at work and to be both productive and effective.

Your thoughts link to your emotions and create the energy level at which you operate and vibrate. It's important to be in control of your emotions so that you can channel them in positive directions. As law of attraction specialist Esther Hicks tells us:

"Nothing is more important than that you feel good."

— Esther Hicks as Abraham

Lifting Your Energy Vibration Levels

 A positive, happy attitude will elevate your energy vibration. By helping your energy pulse at this much higher level, you'll attract more positive people and circumstances into your life. Everything will begin to flow in a more positive manner, and you'll more easily manifest your desires.

Dr. David Hawkins, a psychiatrist, tracked energy vibration levels across the range of emotion in his "Scale of Consciousness." His scale places shame, guilt, apathy, fear, guilt and other negative feelings at the bottom end with an energy vibration rating of 20 at the base.

The scale moves upward toward positive emotions with courage holding the midway point and an energy vibration rating of 200. This point represents a significant shift in one's acceptance, awareness and desire to work toward something better.

The scale moves up to the high end with love at 500, joy at 540, peace at 600 and enlightenment at 700 plus. His scale proves that your inner vibrations really do change based on your positivity and happiness, and the change can be substantial.

Find Ways to Feel Better about Yourself

It doesn't take weeks, months or even years to change your vibrations so you reach the highest levels of Dr. Hawkins' scale. You can think a happy thought right now and see immediate improvement. If you've been mired in negativity for a while, you might be out of practice in finding things to be positive about. Here are some ideas for an instant mood pick-me-up:

- Set aside quality time just for yourself. Indulge in a luxurious bath, get a massage, visit a spa, or just sit by yourself in your favorite outdoor spot.

- Take a restorative afternoon nap just because you want to and you can.

- Go for a long gratitude walk outside, and appreciate the abundance of nature that surrounds you. Observe how nature works effortlessly and think about making your own life as easy.

- Go on a picnic.

- Have a tasty treat by yourself or have coffee, lunch or dinner with a dear friend.

- Listen to music you absolutely love that transports you to a happier place.

- Watch an inspirational, uplifting movie, or read a great book while you curl up on your couch.

- Go out to see a movie or to a sporting event.

- Connect with and support some of your favorite, like-minded virtual friends on Facebook and other social media.

- Set boundaries. Learn to trust yourself and know what's best for you. If people expect too much of you or encroach on your time, define your limits.

- Learn how to say no without guilt. Be honest and forthright and know you don't have to have any particular reason to NOT want to do something.

- Help another person for no reason at all, just because you feel like it. For example:

  - Smile at people as you pass them on the sidewalk. Make eye contact and say a quick "hello." It'll feel good to connect with another person.

  - Be polite and open a door for someone.

  - Ask that cashier how his or her day is going—and then look at them as they answer you to show them that their response matters.

  - Allow someone to go ahead of you in line at the supermarket.

  - When you notice someone trying to get into your lane on the busy freeway, slow down and let them in.

  - Volunteer to help a local community cause, perhaps a soup kitchen. Or contribute your time to help another charitable organization that resonates with you.

- o Put money in someone's parking meter when you see it has expired or is getting very close.

- o Laugh. No—don't chuckle, I mean really guffaw. Nothing spreads positive vibrations through you as quickly as laughter.

You'll be amazed at how much better you feel about yourself when you help others you don't even know. It's priceless and heartening when you see their positive response and it sets the stage for being nicer to yourself.

Take Responsibility for All Areas of Your Life

The first step to becoming a more positive, successful and happy person is to become more personally responsible for all areas of your life.

One of the most important decisions you can make is to take personal responsibility for your life—where you are, what you've done and what you haven't.

When moving toward your goals, there's no blaming others, being a victim of circumstance or pointing the finger. Instead, you must stand up with the belief that you **will** take charge of your life and steer it in the right direction.

Taking responsibility for your own development and progress means increasing your awareness, your knowledge and your ability to evaluate situations and draw conclusions. This is about steering your own journey and not following a guru. This is your journey. You are the one and only person in charge of it.

Each time you take on more responsibility, you peel back another layer and discover more about yourself. Your aim is to become a high-functioning person by owning up, standing up to the plate and taking responsibility for what happens in your life.

You can change your life if you want, and you can be a winner if you choose. You can be the person you want to be but only if you want it enough. Prove that you do by being proactive. Decide today to take full responsibility for all areas of your life.

And remember, taking responsibility doesn't mean you can never ask for help—it means accepting when it's time to ask.

Lifelong Personal Development Education

Your ongoing personal development is a vital component to reaching the level you want in life.

Seeking out self-improvement books and training programs should be an ongoing commitment to learning and bettering yourself. Remember that this is a lifelong journey.

———•◦•———

"There's only one corner of the universe you can be certain of improving, and that's your own self."

— Aldous Huxley

"Rich people have small TVs and big libraries, and poor people have small libraries and big TVs."

— Zig Ziglar

"Formal education will make you a living; self-education will make you a fortune."

—Jim Rohn

———•◦•———

The creation of a successful life evolves from constant, never-ending self-improvement and continual personal progress.

It's not about learning one or two concepts, and then—voila!—you're enlightened and don't have to learn anything else. If it were that easy, everyone would have reached his or her personal pinnacle of victory. Success is a constantly moving target and, thus, centers around constant, unfolding progress.

Take each and every day of the rest of your life and work on yourself first. Continue to learn and study and expand your understanding. As you evolve, attempt to raise the bar even further. As you continue along your journey, you'll find that you're at your most productive and happy when you're learning, growing and developing your knowledge.

Consider this lifelong learning as your quest for truth. In his book, *The Seven Habits of Highly Effective People*, author Stephen Covey talks about developing your mind and thinking. He uses this analogy:

Stop and sharpen the saw and you'll cut through the tree faster.

You don't want to keep grinding away in your career or your personal life. Stop, assess yourself and put effort into self-improvement. Develop your mind, your ability to find a positive perception in any situation and your ability to think clearly.

Cutting Through the Smoke Screen

There are many people in self-help and personal development circles who talk the talk but don't actually walk the walk. It's all a smoke screen, a charade. These people repeat the self-improvement and personal development lessons and lingo but don't actually do the work. I want you to know that I have lived the positive edge. I have watched it make tremendous changes in my life. When I speak to you about all of its tenets, I speak not from theory, but from experience. I don't just give you ideas that might work, I give you a proven method that brought me from employee to owner of multiple million-dollar businesses with an amazing life and rewarding career.

You are here just like I was when I started my journey. You want to honestly do the work, and I know that's your intention. Otherwise, you wouldn't still be reading this book. But when picking out materials to teach and inspire you, do some research on the author and make sure that they represent what they say in their book in all other places.

Recreate the Life You Desire

Novelist George Eliot once said, "It is never too late to be what you might have been." Sounds like great advice, right? And what if you learned that Eliot was actually the pen name of a woman called Mary Ann Evans? You see, Evans knew that in the mid-1800s, one way for a woman to make sure her writing was considered serious was to take on a man's name. Evans took a great risk to realize her full potential. It's unlikely you'll have to go to such great lengths as to hide your gender in order to become what you might have been, but there may be other sacrifices and risks you'll need to take.

You have the power within you to create your life — that ideal life, the one you most desire. If you feel like you've already messed up and are in some inescapable rut, remember that you can recreate your life just as others create theirs. You can develop yourself in any way, and in whatever direction you want. It all starts with a decision: to choose how you experience your life.

The idea that you can create or recreate your life excites me. It makes me want to go out and create more opportunities in my life and do more for others. I want to see just how big and spectacular each of us can make our own existence.

"Once you make a decision, the universe conspires to make it happen."

— Ralph Waldo Emerson

It's amazing how much your beliefs influence the way you perceive things. Earlier we covered the power of your thoughts, beliefs and perceptions and the reality box you've created. The challenge you now face is finding the code to unlocking this box and breaking free from this moment forward. Self-help and self-education offer the combination to unlock and get out of that little box and leave it, once and for all.

Make a commitment to raise your awareness of what you create in your life. There's a bigger picture ahead. We just have to wake up to the reality that we're in control of our lives to a much greater extent than we thought.

With positive thoughts, you give yourself a positive edge to overcome fears, limiting beliefs, self-esteem issues and your poverty consciousness way of thinking.

The future belongs to those who believe in the beauty and wonder held within their dreams. Put one foot in front of the other and remember that achievers and superstars do not listen to the naysayers, saboteurs and doubters. To become one of these superstars, take action and do what needs to be done.

A Word of Caution

There is a big difference between deciding and doing. Deciding isn't doing. Taking action is doing. Don't be lulled or calmed because you *decided* to do something—feel accomplished only after you've actually taken action. Even if it's just a small step— it's still a win for your Victory Journal.

Taking Action Checklist

Are you prepared to take action? Find out by answering all three of these questions. If you answer them yes, then you're ready to go.

1. Have you visualized the action you want to take to get the results you want?

2. Do you think it's reasonable to expect your action to bring about the desired results? For example, if you want to buy one lottery ticket in order to win a million dollars, you're being unreasonable. But if you want to start spending less and saving more, and then invest your savings conservatively, you may be on the right track.

3. Do you believe—meaning, are you absolutely convinced—that you can do this?

Traditionally, people were brought up believing they have to fit into rigid structures and conventional belief systems in order to win. That great success is the result of unbelievable work ethic, genius or luck, that it isn't a simple matter of visualizing, thinking and believing. Yet, that's not what this three-question survey shows. It shows that it really can be simple.

The concept of thinking success into existence is a great counterbalance to the rigid belief that the world is just the way it is, and you can't do anything about it.

Making Yourself Happy

 Creating a life is what makes people happy. The ability to innovate and design the life you want for yourself is where happiness is truly found.

It's a challenge to create your life, sure, but you can also look at it as a game. It's exciting. There will be huge wins, but don't kid yourself: there will also be heartbreaks along the way. Heartbreaks give birth to moving possibilities.

Pursuing the creation of an ideal life is, regardless of heartbreak and missteps, what ultimately makes people happy.

The Power of Choice

We all have the power of choice, but that choice operates within the confines of the real world. You may choose to grow fairy wings and fly around the city catching stars in your hands … but that's not something the universe offers up as a realistic activity.

Within those confines, however, you're in control. That control puts you fairly and squarely at a fork in the road — where you either head toward achieving your goals or toward accepting the status quo, i.e., whatever life throws your way.

Visualize this clearly. It's really important. At every moment, you make a choice and you make decision about how to proceed in that very second. You decide. You choose.

Whether you get up early or sleep in. Whether you make that call or put it off for another day. Whether you write that post for your blog or wait until tomorrow. Whether you write that book now or later. You choose. You decide. It's your free will.

Your decisions and choices, however, have consequences. You can leverage your time and make the most of it, or you can squander it. You can do things now, or "later," a date that very rarely ever arrives.

When you choose the latter, don't be surprised if you haven't achieved much in a year, and almost nothing during the next five years or 20. And don't be surprised if you never live that life you wanted to create.

Take responsibility for your choices and decisions. The words *choose* and *choice* are both incredibly potent. They put you in ultimate control. Exercise this privilege very wisely because these words also suggest an option — the option to have, or have not.

For example:

- You can choose to imagine a successful life or you can choose to see success as something that eludes you.

- You can choose to take action or you can choose idleness in order to avoid the risks and the potential for pain and discomfort.

- You can choose to believe in something grand or you can choose to give up on your grand ideas because everyone around you says you should.

- You can choose to live an active life with increased energy, vibrancy, fitness and health, or you can choose to live a sedentary life and accept the health consequences.

At the end of the day: you must choose to make your life how it will be. You choose by both your action and inaction. You have the power to choose the direction of your life and the results you achieve. No one else can choose for you.

When you see what is possible and within your reach, and believe that it's achievable, you'll want to make it happen. It takes time, effort and resources to turn a worthwhile goal into reality, but the rewards are great once you get there.

What Will You Choose?

What's on your list of things to choose for yourself?

- Success in all areas of my life
- More freedom and independence
- Creating "win-win" scenarios for as many people as I can reach
- Showing and teaching people how to choose more wisely and effectively
- Health, fitness and vibrancy
- Unconditional love

What else would you add to this list?

Choosing to Take Action in Seven Steps

1. Write down at least five areas of your life in which you failed to make **choices** to move forward positively.

2. How much do you want to change that now? Is it possible to start making the change?

3. What can you do to move forward with a different mindset? Write down five action steps—either initial or progressive—for each area you wish to change.

4. Research any special circumstances or considerations surrounding the areas and action steps.

5. Start collecting supplies and support you need in order to take action in the ways you've decided to.

6. Create a deadline for each action step. If you don't, you risk not getting anything done at all.

7. Now, take action and record the results in your Victory Journal.

Get Comfortable with Being Special

 You—yes, you—are more powerful than you believe. You are magical. You are magnificent—but only if you believe you are.

I bet you doubt or disbelieve this at times, maybe even right now. It's exactly this disbelief that's preventing you from living up to your full potential.

Get over it. Give yourself a bit of a shake, breathe deeply and believe from your heart and inner being that you're special and have amazing potential.

To Love Yourself Is to Know Yourself

If you don't know or love yourself, you can't expect others to love you. You have to love and appreciate yourself fully before anyone else can.

You also have to know your purpose and passion, as they're both connected—they are who *you* are.

Once you get to know yourself, you'll begin to understand what your personal passions are. Since your purpose drives your passions, you can work backward to figure it out.

Passion, Purpose and the Higher Self

Do you know what your life's purpose or passion is? At this stage, many people say they don't, but deep within them an answer burns that they're too scared to say out loud.

If you aren't certain that you've discovered your purpose and passion, that's okay. You'll become positive when you find that you're naturally exuberant about something, when you're doing what you love and it flows.

Your purpose is the whole reason you're here. It's a special role, talent or skill you're predisposed to, or special contribution you make that drives you. Often it's something that improves the lives of other people.

Your passion is what you love doing, what excites you. It's that activity you'd give anything to do. It's something that keeps you moving forward, no matter how often you get knocked down. It supplies an endless source of energy, interest and concentration and becomes your driving force.

Passion is what fills the mold of your ideal life. Once the mold is at capacity, serendipity steps in and circumstances fall into place. It's like a "wind at your back" factor that comes from behind and pushes you forward.

When things fall into place quickly and easily, you know that's what's happening. When you do what you love, you're driven, guided by divine intuition and gut instinct. Time flies, and it won't even be an effort. You'll be hyperfocused, almost in a trancelike state. People and resources will simply show up in your day to help you achieve your vision and goals.

Your North Star

Some refer to the direction you're heading in as your North Star. This drive and motivation acts like a compass to set you on a particular course, giving you greater vision, aim and focus.

In her book, *Finding Your North Star: Claiming the Life You Were Meant to Live*, Martha Beck talks about pursuing your North Star. It's interesting to look at an analogy in shipping, yachting and sailing—observe your compass and turn your ship to head due north. Your "turn" may be exemplified in action or in spirit.

As you discover your North Star, you'll feel its power pulling you in a particular direction. If you resist and play it safe, your life won't change very much, if at all. Allow your ideal future self to guide and coach you. Make sure that what you're creating is in tune with your higher self, your own personal greater good.

When you're tuned to that, you'll feel right and will have a strong gut instinct. Things will flow. People and resources will appear to support you.

Know What You Want—and Why You Want It

When speaking with people from all walks of life, either in my business or my personal life, I'm constantly amazed at how many don't know what they really want out of life.

When I ask them, some people say, "I don't really know," as though they've never stopped to think about it. Others say, "I just want to be happy." While this is certainly a clear *want*, it's buried in such a broad, directionless message that they will never actually get there.

Those who get what they want out of life are different. They are very clear and specific about what they want and their reasons why.

It's the reasons behind your goals and desires that motivate you, driving you toward success. Having goals without motives is like having a limo without a chauffeur. If you want to reach your destination, you've got to have a driver, and motives are the drivers that get you to your goals. If you aren't sure what goals you have, if nothing immediately jumps to the forefront of your mind, then you need to think about what makes you feel excited and happy.

It can be overwhelming when faced with the notion that you are able to do anything. After all, anything is a lot of things, isn't it? It's like going to the grocery store and having to choose between 800 types of cereal, none of which you've eaten before. Instead of allowing this to overwhelm you, just start finding things that make you feel really happy—giddy, even—and allow them to guide you to your goals.

Reason doesn't just help you stay on task, it also stokes any inner desires you have—and those are powerful motivators to keep you going.

Finding Your Motivations in Seven Steps

1. Write down a very clear description of what you *don't* want. This is a great way to narrow down the possibilities. Once you know what these things are, you can turn your back on them completely.

2. Write down a very clear description of what you *do* want. This doesn't have to be goals but can be a picture of your ideal lifestyle, career and so on.

3. Write down the reasons why you *don't* want those items or situations you wrote down for step #1.

4. Write down the reasons why you *do* want those items or situations you wrote down for step #2. Your reasons must be compelling and meaningful to you. They'll be what motivate you to get out of bed in the morning and jump enthusiastically into your day with a sense of purpose.

5. What personal passions are connected to what you *do* want?

6. Create one purpose statement for each of your wants. Think of it like a mission statement for each goal.

7. Begin thinking about the action steps you can take to reach your goals and fulfill your reasons.

Are You Ready to Discover What You Want?

There's one thing you were born to do. This thing taps into your unique, natural abilities and will help you create a meaningful, contribution-based life and career that's both fulfilling and financially rewarding.

You have two lives: the one you're living and the unlived life that's within you. Right now, it's time to close the gap.

Resistance

Resistance is what resides in the space between the real and the ideal. It presents itself as disbelief, procrastination and a host of other counterproductive attitudes that end up sabotaging your chance at success. Sadly, it doesn't actually present itself when it should.

You might think it's completely innocent when you decide to take a nap, snooze a little longer, watch TV or have junk food or that extra glass of wine or beer. Since there's little to no inner resistance, you simply indulge yourself and feel good about it.

Instead, resistance presents itself when you're called to do things that matter to your future—things that allow you to step up and achieve your true purpose and full potential.

It's very easy to get sidetracked from the process of discovering your purpose and passion. After all, there are more things available to sidetrack you than there are to inspire you. But you must break through the resistance to unearth these vital pieces of yourself. Remember, that thing you've been waiting for is already inside you. You're already equipped to live a full, rich life. If you aren't doing so, it's by choice, whether conscious or subconscious.

Each of us has a responsibility to make our ideal life happen, to make our dreams happen, to find our purpose and integrate our passions, and pursue them.

———•◆•———

"Our greatest purpose in life is to align with what makes our heart sing."

— Emmanuel Dagher

147

Finding Your Passion in Seven Steps

1. What excites you? Include passive activities as they can often lead you to understanding what you'd like to do with your life and career.

2. What activities motivate you and make you feel happy?

3. What do you find easy and natural to do?

4. What are your skills and your strengths?

5. What have you always dreamed of doing?

6. What would you do if you knew you couldn't fail?

7. What's that special thing you've always wanted to do?

The answers to each of these questions lead you to your passions. Your main passions are those that appear woven into the most answers.

Once you've identified your passions, use some of the other exercises, such as the Taking Action exercise in Chapter 5, to figure out how to funnel your passions into your purpose.

Integrity and Authenticity

You can't live your ideal life if you're ever untrue to your authentic self. The basis of all these lessons is to be positive and believe in what you're doing—and you can't do either if you're living a lie.

Why waste your life working toward a goal that doesn't really represent who you truly are? You have to be true to yourself every step of the way and stay vigilant so that you don't get sidetracked.

Know yourself, and who you are; be self-confident and proud to be uniquely you. After all, that's the most precious commodity you have.

Making a Habit of Happiness and Joy

 It's important to have fun and enjoy yourself whether you're at work or play. It's great to increase your education and learn new methods of working, but you also want to be entertained at the same time. Our natural instinct is to be happy. Happiness is directly related to how much fun we're having. Let's make

having fun a priority each day and incorporate it as a very powerful positive habit.

Begin each day by asking yourself, "What will I do today to have some fun and make myself happy?" Have lunch with a friend, or find a way to have a good, hearty laugh. Play a silly email trivia game with your coworkers or give yourself an hour or two to read. Just have fun!

Esther Hicks, when channeling Abraham, talks about positivity as if it were a seed. She uses the analogy that you plant positivity and allow it to pollinate and bloom, filling your personal garden with the beautiful flowers it creates.

I like to think that happiness and joy are the blooms of positivity. They require positivity just as gardenias require sunlight, soil and water. They need care just like any flower bed. You must weed out negative influences that threaten to choke your precious blooms. You must nourish them when the soil becomes too arid. Happiness and joy are the perennials of your life's garden. Take time each and every day to stop and enjoy them.

We live in a fast-paced world and there never seems to be enough time to fit in everything we want to do. Everything is high pressure, stress, work and more work. But it all amounts to nothing if you don't fit happiness and joy into your days.

Every morning, make it a habit to ask yourself, "What will I do today to have fun and make myself happy?" Just playing with the options will bring a smile to your face. Go ahead; see what happens when you actually ask the question.

When you're happy, serotonin releases into your system. Often called the happiness hormone, serotonin actually isn't a hormone but a neurotransmitter. It plays a role in the regulation of several nervous system functions, including mood, sleep, appetite and learning.

Endorphins are a hormone and peptide that function as neurotransmitters. These are stimulated when you're active and moving your body. Together, serotonin and endorphins help to make you happy. To combine the two, find a fun activity and you'll get happiness squared.

"Very little is needed to make a happy life; it is all within yourself, in your way of thinking."

— Marcus Aurelius

"Be the happy in someone's happy day."

— Karen Salmansohn

"Life, liberty and the pursuit of happiness."

— United States Declaration of Independence

 Developing the Habit of Fun in Seven Steps

1. Write down as many fun activities as you can think of. Remember—these activities need to be things that _you_ enjoy. Make sure some of them include an aspect of physicality so you can take advantage of those endorphins.

2. Write down activities you've not tried but that look fun and interesting.

3. Write down your daily commitment to indulge in at least one of the fun activities you've written down. Choose a regular time every day that you'll dedicate to fun.

4. Make a joyful playlist. Put together songs that make you smile in spite of yourself. This list could include children's music, gospel, parody songs or something you remember from your teen years—the point is to find tunes that bring a grin to your face. You can listen to this music anytime you need a quick pick-me-up.

5. Download pictures and videos you love and put them on your computer and mobile devices. When you need an instant lift, watch the video and receive a happiness injection.

6. Create a screensaver filled with pictures that make you smile.

7. Search out new fun material each week—from pictures to videos, music to activities.

Gratitude and Positive Power

 One of the biggest favors you can do for yourself is to cultivate a daily habit of gratitude. It's really easy, and totally fulfilling. All it involves is acknowledging all the wonderful things you already have in your life.

Never underestimate what you already have. Give thanks, be grateful and always count your blessings. Happiness will not come to those who don't appreciate what they have.

When you're grateful and appreciative, you lift your energy to a higher vibration level. It keeps you firmly focused on the positives in your life. Following the law of attraction and quantum physics principles, this attracts even more of what you value and appreciate.

Developing the Habit of Gratitude in Seven Steps

1. Write down five constants in your life that you're grateful for. Take notice of the kinds of things that pop up in your mind when you consider what you consistently have to be thankful for.

2. Every morning when you wake, write down those things you're grateful to look forward to, from that first cup of coffee to an exciting lunch date, to the use of your new stapler.

3. Every afternoon, write down at least one unexpected event or incident that has made you feel grateful that day.

155

4. Every evening, before taking the first bite of your dinner, express gratitude for the fact that you have food and can sit and enjoy it. Make note of these in your Gratitude Journal.

5. Before bed, write down at least one thing that happened during the afternoon and evening that made you feel grateful.

6. Once each week, take stock of any life changes that made you feel grateful.

7. Once each month, take stock of the world around you and write down at least one large-scale thing you're grateful for.

Become Your Ideal Future Self

For the last several pages, we've focused on truly dialing into your ideal self. Now that you know that part of yourself better, it's time to think about integrating this self into your current life.

A future self is only the future version of you if you aren't trying to become them now. You've spent a lot of years with that ideal person standing in the periphery of your vision— now it's time to open the door to your life and let that ideal self take the driver's seat.

Remember, your ideal self isn't some alien pod person who always smiles and does the right thing. You're not cultivating a Stepford wife. The ultimate goal is to always be yourself—but not the *you* you've been told to be or the *you* your negative thoughts convinced you that you were. You want to be the real you, the confident, proud, passionate and purposeful you.

As you project forward and connect with your ideal future self, allow your instincts to become your expert advisor, guiding you along the way.

 ## Define Your Ideal Future Self in Seven Steps

1. In your Victory Journal, write a thorough description of you once you've become completely integrated with your ideal self. Talk about your clothes, the look on your face, the way you carry yourself and so on.

2. Now, write down the qualities and traits that you possess as your ideal future self. Think of things such as courage, drive, determination, trust, confidence and so on.

3. Write down the accomplishments you've achieved as your ideal future self. These can be actual awards and promotions or they can be inner, personal accomplishments.

4. What do your future friends and associates look and act like once you've reached your ideal?

5. How does it make you feel to visualize all these aspects of your future life? It should make you feel excited, determined and ready. If it makes you feel scared or hesitant, you may want to review the sections on fears and being authentic.

6. If you talked to your future self as you are today, and told them that your goal was to become them, what advice would they give you to get started? What direction would they share?

7. Create an action plan to integrate all those aspects of your future self—which you already possess—into your current life. Include steps such as acting the part, improving your attitude, taking risks and so on. Be specific and assign timelines to achieve these action plan goals.

Being Yourself

There's no time like the present to start being the person you want to be. Many people have it the wrong way around. They think that first you have to **do**, then you will **have**, and then eventually you will **be**.

In fact, it works the other way around — *be* who you want to be, do as that person would do, and **then** you'll have what you want. This is one of the most basic personal development concepts. It's been around for a very long time ... at least a few thousand years.

It's also a basic concept that captures the very essence of being human: being alive, living that life and creating results. It's as simple as that.

The prerequisite to the be/do/have philosophy is to take responsibility for your life and your results — or lack thereof.

Being means finding your own individual identity. You do this separately from everyone else, regardless of what they think, agree with and believe. You develop this understanding of yourself away from any other influence, such as what your parents thought of you during childhood or the insults kids hurled at you in high school. It's not about the outside world, but the inside world.

When it comes to getting results, it's not about feeling as though you have to like and please everyone. It's also not about creating some ultimate harmony. It's about finding your own heart, your own purpose, your knowledge, and having the confidence to live those truths independently. When you reach this level and live it, not only will you see how you fit into the larger scheme of things, you'll also become more effective in helping others and showing them how they can pursue a better life.

Moving Toward Win-Win

In the past few years there's been a noticeable shift toward a more heart-centered approach to business. This involves a focus on integrity and accountability while supporting the pursuit of passion.

Taking a cold, calculating approach toward doing business is becoming more and more frowned upon. Not only does that benefit each of us as consumers but as professionals and business owners as well. A heart-centered approach allows you to connect with the true desire to help people and enjoy a more collaborative, interactive, life-enriching experience.

Being of service to others is a most noble and fulfilling motivation and purpose. When you can merge this service-based attitude with your purpose and your passion, every day is a joy. This is the ideal win-win situation that brings even more positivity flowing your way.

"You will get all you want in life if you help enough other people get what they want."

— Zig Ziglar

Creating win-win situations is also a concept in Steven Covey's *The Seven Habits of Highly Effective People*. The ultimate point of this heart-centered path is that your life is not all about you. You may want to win for yourself, but that's simply not possible without ensuring wins for people around you. This is a positive step forward because you can't succeed for too long if you're the only person winning.

Aim to build something that benefits you and those around you—a genuine win-win for everyone concerned.

Chapter 6:

Designing Your Support System

The most important aspect of gaining the positive edge is to feel good—happy, joyful, optimistic—every day. But there's one thing that can completely stand in the way of your doing that, and that is having a bad support system surrounding you.

Likability

There's no question that if you want to be liked, you have to be likable. It makes sense, really. In this book, we've talked a lot about how positivity attracts more positive things and energy to you. Think about that in terms of the relationships you have. When you're positive and fun and outgoing, you attract more of the same type of people to you.

Have you ever been around someone who's pessimistic? Someone who's gloomy, negative and sees only bad things? If you have, I bet you've dreaded seeing the person again. And as mean as that sounds, it's totally rational. It's just like the snowball effect of the positive edge—this person's negativity picks up other negativity and gathers into a black cloud of pessimism. That's not the right environment for you, and it's not the kind of group that others will want to join either.

If you want to create a support system that works for you, one that helps pull you out of the doldrums when you need it or that helps you stay focused and on point to your goals, then you need to be likable.

 Being Likable in Seven Steps

1. Ask your friends and family members to list out three of your best qualities and three of your worst.

2. Review the answers you received. Are there any common threads? What do these commonalities tell you must be changed? What are you doing right?

3. Think about the negative traits pointed out to you. Do you notice these things about yourself? Are you willing to change them?

4. For those traits you're willing to change, come up with a plan. Write out the gradual adjustments you'll make to them each week or month.

5. Learn to listen more than you talk. People like those who make eye contact with them and actually listen to what they say.

6. Work on staying positive. People like others who are uplifting, fun and enjoyable to be around—not those who complain all the time.

7. Use your Victory Journal to write down all the victories your likability changes bring. Review these entries to remind you of the difference it makes when you're well liked.

Charisma

There are people who have a certain spark, an almost indefinable shine that draws others in. This is charisma. You'll know someone is charismatic because they're like a magnet, attracting all the other people at the party or in the room.

Being charismatic isn't required in order to gain the positive edge, but it can help. Charismatic people inspire fierce loyalty in their network and they have a knack for attracting major opportunities to themselves.

 ### *Being More Charismatic in Seven Steps*

1. Be comfortable with you. Charismatic people do not hold back. They trust in themselves and allow their inner light to shine outward. You must be completely comfortable with who you are before you can do that. Here is an exercise that can help you get over fears of being yourself.

- o Write down all the ways you're scared to fully be you.
- o Write down the worst that can happen if your fears come true.
- o Now think about the likelihood of those worst-case scenarios actually happening.

2. Let your passion rise to the surface. Charismatic people are passionate about the things they take on, and they imbue everything they do with that zest. If you're passionate, allow that to come out more often.

3. Watch your body language. Charismatic people don't slouch, they don't cross their arms, they don't slink in a corner—they

want to be the center of attention. Not for their ego, but because they're having fun. Speaking of which …

4. Learn how to have fun. I've never met a boring charismatic person. I've also never met one who couldn't have fun in almost any environment. If you want to develop charisma, you need to let yourself have a good time.

5. Enjoy other people. People enjoy being around charismatic people because they make them feel good. But one of the ways they do that is by being interested and enjoying the people around them.

6. Be trustworthy. If everyone thinks your charisma is an act, and if you don't follow through on the things you say, then you're not going to inspire loyalty. Be truthful and trustworthy.

7. Get comfortable speaking in public. You have to be outgoing and gregarious to be charismatic. Practice your public speaking and storytelling skills.

Controlling Your Circle

Friendships and relationships are the one place where we tend to focus more on feelings than goals. This can be a problem if your feelings of sentimentality lead you to keep someone around who will sabotage your goals. If you have a negative employee, limit the influence they have over the office. Negative friends and family members need to also have limited access to you and your life. In some cases, you may even want to end the relationship if it causes you more harm than it's worth.

One way to evaluate the way that a relationship affects you is to journal after spending time with the person. Write about how you feel after being with them and whether the feelings are helpful to your positive edge lifestyle.

Building a Network of Positivity

In my experience, most people fall into one of two categories: either worrying about achieving more than others for fear of rejection or not caring about that a single bit.

Quite frankly, if people react negatively, critically or cynically to your success, it may be time to reassess your friends and associates.

It could be that they're jealous because they're no longer perceived as more successful than you. Or maybe they are resentful because they've never reached your level of success. It doesn't really matter the reason behind their feelings—if people are that small-minded and petty and can't spare any positive words about your success, do you really want to have them around you? Do you want them influencing your life and decisions? Changing your perception of their role in your life is a great way to throw off the shackles they put on you and head guilt-free toward your success.

Don't let these people hold you back. You may think you simply can't cut them out of your life, as it might seem ruthless and cold, but it isn't. You're taking care of your best interests. You're setting your boundaries and supporting your healthy self-esteem. You're looking after yourself, your time, your focus and priorities. You deserve a proper support system that includes positive people and a giving, back-and-forth environment. Consider what Warren Buffet asks himself of people whose business he considers investing in:

1. "Do I like them?"

2. "Do I trust them?"

3. "Do I respect them?"

As you age, the people in your life come and go. You attract new like-minded friends and acquaintances who help you grow further. It's evolution. And remember, your success and income is a reflection of the five closest people in your life so, choose your friends wisely.

"You are the average of the five people you spend the most time with."

— Jim Rohn

Chapter 7:
Take Action One Step at a Time

One of the greatest benefits to living a positive edge lifestyle is that even if you go slow, taking it just one step at a time, you will still find benefits flowing toward you immediately. And even more come as you progress forward.

There's nothing overwhelming or unachievable with the positive edge; the entire goal of the program is to make sure you stack the odds in favor of your success.

Maintain a Firm Vision

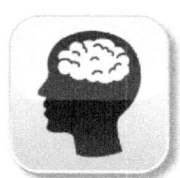 To move forward the right way, do so with self-assurance and keep hold of your vision at all times. Heading in the right direction really has to do with deciding what you want, deciding

where you want to go (or what you want your life to look like) and setting your compass to get there. It's all about choosing to go in that single direction you've set your sights on.

In our lives we take on a lot of baggage, limiting beliefs and responsibilities. Negative attitudes surround us. These factors tend to wear down our confidence, and when we allow that, it becomes impossible to move forward toward our vision and goals.

You must choose not to let those anchors weigh you down and instead, take action to move forward. Every step you take should bring you closer to your ideal life. It doesn't matter if you're taking big steps or small—just make sure you aren't treading water. Each progressive move should push you closer to your desired destination.

Inspiration and Motivation

Inspiration and motivation are often what get you started and what maintain your spirits when you're struggling, so it's important to understand what they are and how they're generated.

Inspiration is where vision comes from. It's probably happened to you a thousand times, but you've just never put the two together. You see, learn, experience or hear something that inspires you and then, suddenly, your creative juices flow and your head fills with ideas. Like popcorn kernels over a heat source, your concepts start bouncing and crowding each other out as they blossom into vision.

But without motivation, your inspiration and vision will be nothing but a pretty picture in your head. Like a creativity hangover, you'll be left tired, unwell and completely unfulfilled. That's why you need motivation.

Motivation is what drives you to take action and maintain your forward momentum. But it can wane. We are, after all, only human.

Motivation tends to be driven more often by the external and tangible. We look for positive reinforcement that we're on the right track, doing the right thing, and going about it all the right way. This reinforcement might come in the form of feedback from others or from something more tangible, such as money coming in through our efforts. Either of these scenarios (and many others) motivates us further and keeps our energy pumping along, allowing our visions to come to fruition.

Here are three things you can do when you find your motivation waning:

- Solicit feedback about how you're doing and progressing.

- Implement action steps and tick them off as you go.

- Measure your results.

Inspiration is the starting point to motivation. It's that idea that you can attain what you've envisioned that helps you take those vital first few steps.

Set Your Intentions for Tomorrow

If I could only give you one tip that will absolutely change your life and increase activity by an enormous amount, it would be to plan your next day the night before. Every evening before you fall asleep, set your intentions for the following day. By doing this, you give an assignment to your subconscious mind to work on while you sleep.

Allowing your subconscious to kick the day's plans around before you get up in the morning will also help you resolve some of the issues that may be worrying you and preventing actual achievement. This will then give you suggestions for clearing the path to more easily achieving what you want.

 ## Setting Intentions in Seven Steps

1. Every night, think about the things you want to get done, get started or continue working on the following day.

2. Write these down along with a goal for how much of each you intend to accomplish.

3. Create a daily activity guide with three or more absolute MUST-DO daily activities that never change.

4. In the morning upon waking, review your intentions and your daily activities. Read them out loud.

5. Repeat aloud several visualizations and affirmations that motivate and inspire confidence.

6. After repeating your affirmations, visualize writing down each of your completed tasks as accomplishments in your Victory Journal.

7. Believe that you can accomplish it all and get ready to take action.

Visualizing the Life You Want

 Visualizing is a big part of the process of creating your ideal life. It helps involve your emotions, which are very strong influencers.

Affirmations on their own don't always work. Because they don't yet represent realities, your subconscious may hold some disbelief. However, affirmations combined with visualizations work more effectively.

 Visualization in Seven Steps

1. Start by honing your visualization skills. Choose a scenario—time, place, setting—and visualize yourself there. See yourself moving around in the space, picking things up, smiling and interacting with others.

2. Loosen up so that you may begin to have real feelings during your visualization. Imagine amazing, wonderful things and feel your chest expand with joy.

3. Incorporate your other senses. Introduce a pleasant smell into your visualization—lavender, your spouse's cologne or even the scent of hot tar. Layer in some sounds—birds chirping,

water rushing, traffic going by, music—anything you want. Next, visualize putting your hand on something warm and feel the heat. Or something soft or sticky. Make it a sensory experience, as it will have a greater impact.

4. Ask yourself questions as you visualize. The questions you ask can include: How does this visualization make me feel? What more would I like to feel and experience? Why do I want this?

5. Design a visualization that will help you accomplish something. Make it something small, such as a phone call you've been dreading. Imagine yourself walking to the phone, holding the cool, smooth receiver in your hand, pushing it against your ear. Feel your fingers dialing the number, hear it ring, listen to the voice on the other end. Make sure you feel good during the process, so it helps the reality of making the call seem less daunting.

6. The next day, write down how it felt to actually accomplish what you visualized the previous day. Be sure to record this as a win in your Victory Journal.

7. Put visualization on your daily activity plan. Make it an absolute must. It's best to practice at the beginning of your day. Remember, the goal of the activity is to focus your thoughts on visualizing things, events, situations, places and people that make you feel great.

Asking Quality Questions

Noah St. John also tells us about "afformations," which are questions rather than stated affirmations. These questions mobilize your brain to actively find the answers. They have more power than affirmations, which may be a bit of a stretch to believe in your current circumstances.

Often, a question is the simple seed that starts a change in your life. Questions seem innocuous, but really, they're vital to our overall growth. The spark of curiosity that they represent catches fire and that fire becomes the burning desire that pushes you to make a change.

It stands to reason, then, that your quality of life is determined by the value of questions you ask yourself. If you ask yourself easy questions—those that require no thought or effort, no challenge or personal investment—you suppress your inner spark and allow yourself to skate by living a shallow life.

The quality of your questions can hold you back or propel you toward the success, happiness and fulfillment you've been seeking. Asking yourself quality questions prompts your mind to go searching to find the answers. Try it and see.

Here's an example of a shallow question versus a quality question:

1. What do I have as proof of my success? (shallow)

2. Why am I successful? (quality)

Why is the first question considered shallow? Think of it this way: it's much easier to list the proof of your success than it is to drill down and discover how and *why* it came to be. While the first question would be answered with a list of results, the second can only be answered by understanding the amazing, powerful traits you hold. When you ask yourself quality questions, your mind automatically goes searching for the reasons WHY, which serves to reinforce your confidence and inspire you to keep moving forward. Try it out—it's more empowering and believable.

 ## Quality Questions in Seven Steps

1. Write a list of **quality questions** to ask yourself.

For example:

- What are my best skills?

- What are my best qualities?

- What is the next best action I can take? Why?

- What actions will get me where I wish to go?

- Why am I so abundant?

- Why am I so successful?

- Why do I have such productive and cooperative relationships?

- What is the most important thing I can do today? (See next section for more on this important question.)

Add any other questions that come to mind.

2. Consider these questions one at a time and write down your answers.

3. Make a note of any that are uncomfortable for you to answer—this is usually a good sign of a quality question.

4. Take some of the shallow questions you've been asking yourself and turn them into quality questions.

5. Answer your new quality questions and see how big a difference you find in the answers compared to when you were asking shallow questions.

6. Write down some ways you can tell a shallow question from a quality question, based on your unique experience.

7. How will you prevent yourself from asking shallow questions in the future? Write the answer down in your journal.

The Most Important Thing to Do Today

Each day, when you wake up, you should ask yourself: *What is the most important thing I can do today?* Or, *What is the most important action step I can take?* The answer should directly benefit you or something you care about. Asking these questions will help you define priorities in your life.

The answer does not have to be big or complex, but it will help you set your compass and focus on what really matters in your life.

The Importance of Sustained Action

Taking action is amazing and powerful, but sustained action is what gets you through the long haul and into the life of your dreams. Look at Facebook, as an example. This was a site that started in out 2004 as a way for Harvard students to privately connect with others at their school and now it's visited by 400 million people each month. Here's the secret to significant, long-term success: Take action now, keep it going with heaps of short-term activities, and sustain it with repeated action on a continuous, persistent basis over the long term.

"Success is the sum of small efforts, repeated day in and day out."

— Robert Collier

Short-Term Action and Long-Term Action

One important ingredient in creating a successful life and business is to commit to making short-term actions. Once you create the habit of making these short-term moves, they gain momentum and evolve into long-term actions.

Only through repetition and sustained action will you achieve results. Generate the determination and drive necessary to sustain your efforts over the long-term and you can accomplish anything. It's a test of your endurance, energy and ultimate belief in yourself.

Results: 90 Days or Less

There's almost nothing as gratifying as a small dose of immediate gratification. It's part of what makes the positive edge so fun—most people begin to see small results *immediately*. Just by adopting a more positive outlook, life becomes more fulfilling. Bigger results usually begin in about 90 days. By then, your actions have begun to build momentum, creating a force of their own.

After you begin to see results, it's important to commit to back-to-back 90-day plans in order to really work the program, drill into your desires and obstacles, and get the most out of your life.

By doing back-to-back plans of 90-day intervals, you put a mechanism in place to help sustain your efforts and maintain momentum. This is an important link in the chain because once you lose momentum, you have to start all over again.

To achieve in a big way, make this program your top priority for the very first 90-day period. In subsequent periods, it can play more of a background role; however, you must devote time to focusing and asking quality questions of yourself in order to drill into those steps and push yourself. Remember, the quality of your returns is commensurate to the quality of the effort you put in.

When you know your big-picture vision and you have a plan, keep your roadmap simple. Make it a rule to implement at least one action step per day. Remember what I said earlier—it's all about each individual step. Don't overwhelm yourself by trying to do everything at once. Quality effort breeds quality results—give yourself the ability to complete the steps the right way.

When attempting a program that's designed to change their lives, too many people give up too soon, lose interest or do the start-stop-start dance. It's easy to get distracted, grow bored or lose faith. The thing is, if you're inconsistent, it will never take.

The clear message is: keep going no matter what, and avoid stopping and starting over again.

 ## Committing to the Positive Edge Lifestyle in Seven Steps

1. Make a personal commitment to stick to your plan over the long haul.

2. List things you can do that will keep you focused, energized and committed to sustaining action.

3. Write down ways you plan to motivate yourself should you become distracted or discouraged.

4. Keep track and record your wins in your Victory Journal. Remember to include each time you applied consistent and sustained actions on a daily basis.

5. Create a 90-day plan for yourself. This should include a daily schedule of activities devoted to the program.

6. Design a modified plan for the next 90-day period.

7. Review your results at the end of each 90-day period and record what you learned, what worked, what didn't work, what you will do next and how you'll modify and improve your next 90-day period.

Perseverance, Consistency and Commitment

Successful people share three traits that set them apart from the crowd: perseverance, consistency and commitment. Unfortunately, most people aren't born with the qualities of perseverance and consistency. These characteristics have to be developed, especially if you want to master your new skills and talents, endow yourself with a sustainable advantage and stack your odds in favor of success.

We all have our good and bad days, highs and lows, ups and downs. Some people are predisposed to feeling down depending on their upbringing, personalities, emotions, beliefs, habits and circumstances. That's what makes perseverance such an important trait—perseverance makes it possible to carry on through the bad times. Commitment breeds perseverance, and perseverance brings consistency. That means you must be committed to persevering—even when you feel bad. This will help you keep consistent and get that positivity growth we've been talking about.

Success is not an accident. It's not luck. It requires constant motion and application, energy, enthusiasm and conviction. Not everyone gets the results they desire and set out to achieve. This is because they don't stick with it. People give up, sometimes when they're right on the edge of success. The clear message is to absolutely never give up. You have no idea what's around the next bend.

———————●◆●———————

"Our greatest weakness lies in giving up. The most certain way to succeed is always to try just one more time."

— Thomas Edison

"Anyone can give up; it's the easiest thing in the world to do. But to hold it together when everyone else would understand if you fell apart, that's true strength."

— Unknown

"Most people give up just when they're about to achieve success. They quit on the one-yard line. They give up at the last minute of the game one foot from a winning touchdown."

— Ross Perot

"Nothing in this world can take the place of persistence. Talent will not; nothing is more common than unsuccessful people with talent. Genius will not; unrewarded genius is almost a proverb. Education will not; the world is full of educated failures. Persistence and determination alone are omnipotent."

— Calvin Coolidge

Progress and Flexibility

It's important to stay open to the possibilities rather than being fixed and obstinate. Only with flexibility will you be able to make the changes necessary to progress.

Don't be disheartened if things don't initially work as you'd hoped. Learn from the experience and adopt new methods as needed. Your knowledge is growing and deepening. Making changes and trying again allows you to improve your odds. Keep doing that, and your time will come.

Getting Organized and Getting Things Done

Being disorganized can create stress and confusion, which leads to a feeling of being overwhelmed. This is completely draining and takes time from the things you want to do.

Disorganization is a high-cost lifestyle to maintain. Its expenses include time, opportunity, success, productivity, pride and confidence. It can even cost you money through late charges, lost discounts, health issues and more.

When you think of a disorganized person, you may imagine someone who has mounds of paper, unopened envelopes, piled-up newspapers, stacks of laundry and so on. While that does fit the definition, we now also have a new digital disorganization causing problems. This can be seen through overflowing inboxes, downloaded data, overloaded data limits, documents that are all over the place, unorganized bookmarks and lost passwords. Both forms of disorganization create discomfort and anxiety.

A cluttered environment doesn't lend itself to personal betterment and success. What you see in your living and working environments is a reflection of what's in your head, which is why you must devote time to getting organized and staying that way.

It actually takes less time and effort to do things when you're already organized and decluttered than when your home, office and mind are a mess.

Time and energy are precious. Efficiency is the key to maximizing those limited and valuable commodities and accomplishing all you set out to do.

Organizing and Decluttering in Seven Steps

Here's a simple system you can follow. It doesn't have to be complicated. Start applying these steps, one at a time.

1. Write down all the cleaning, organizing and decluttering tasks you want to get done today. Remember, you don't have to get your whole home or office done in a single day. It took you years to make the mess; it might take days or weeks to clean it up. Try to focus on one room at a time or, if that's too overwhelming, one area at a time.

2. Assign a specific block of time for completing each task on the list.

3. Begin with your first task. Set a time and focus on nothing else until that chore is complete. Then, move on to the next item on the to-do list.

4. For bigger tasks, such as cleaning out a large filing cabinet, break down the project into bite-sized portions and do each, one at a time, until the steps are completed. For example, you may choose to clean out just one drawer of the cabinet each day for four days.

5. Don't neglect any aspect of your life. Include your home, office, car, shed, computer and garage in this overhaul. Even if it takes you a year to fully renovate your life, it's worth it.

6. Organize in a way that makes sense to you and don't be afraid to take notes about your process. Disorganized people very often fall back into old habits simply because they forget what their logic was behind a certain approach.

7. Develop a maintenance schedule. At the end of each day, you should devote time to making sure everything is put back in its place. Additionally, you'll need to work out a weekly or monthly schedule for organizing things like mail, email and papers for filing.

The Pareto Principle

We all do things each day to contribute to our success, but some of the things we do are more effective than others. The Pareto Principle, or 80-20 rule, recommends that you focus your efforts on the 20 percent of activities that give you 80 percent of your results.

It makes sense to focus on what will give you maximum results. Using this principle when planning your actions will maximize the time and effort you spend on various tasks and bring you the most bang for your buck.

Effective Time Management

If you don't manage your time with clarity and purpose, you'll leave yourself vulnerable and end up sucked into events and dramas that don't serve any purpose in your ultimate goal. This will take control of your time and significantly dilute your power. One of the most effective tactics to manage your time and avoid feeling overwhelmed is to understand that you are an important, all-powerful person in charge of your own time, priorities and schedule.

You set your boundaries. You and you alone get to decide when to say yes, and when to say no. No one can encroach upon your time without your permission.

Time Management in Seven Steps

1. Set strict and specific boundaries and stick to them religiously. You don't owe anyone an explanation, but you do owe yourself dedication.

For example, don't answer your phone during preset blocks of time you've allocated to other tasks. Return calls later when it's convenient.

Don't jump as soon as the phone rings because doing so hands over power to the phone, at your expense.

2. Be aware of time as a limited commodity and schedule designated blocks to undertake and complete tasks.

3. Use the time management quadrant:

Set up a document or table on your computer (or a piece of paper) with four quadrants. Name the quadrants from left to right, 1 and 2 at the top, 3 and 4 directly underneath. Label as:

1. Urgent and Important

2. Urgent, but Not Important

3. Not Urgent, but Important

4. Not Urgent and Not Important

Slot your priorities into the appropriate quadrant to gain clarity, control and focus over the day ahead.

4. Avoid the seductive email inbox.

Opening your email can feel like pulling the arm of a slot machine—what amazing wonders await you inside? Money? Fame? Prizes? If you want to maintain control of your day rather than having your emails control it, resist the temptation to open mail first thing in the morning.

If you're expecting something time sensitive, simply scan the box for the individual who will be sending that reply, but don't look at any of the other emails. Instead, pick a time in the afternoon when your focus wanes and you can't concentrate on more pressing tasks. Limit yourself to spending 15 minutes on email during that period.

5. Use your out-of-office reply and your voicemail. It's difficult to ignore the phone and email. Often, you feel as though you'll

lose business or opportunities if you do. To ease some of this anxiety, have messages prepared that state you will be unavailable until a certain time and that you'll return calls and emails when you're back at your desk.

6. Write down a schedule for your day. Sometimes it helps to have a schedule of tasks with time allotments. When you make these kinds of appointments with yourself, you're better able to guard your time.

7. Utilize the Pomodoro Technique. The Pomodoro Technique is a time management method that limits your focus on a single activity to 25-minute blocks. You can use a kitchen or other timer to measure these blocks.

At the end of the 25 minutes, a five-minute break is taken to get you up and away from your computer and your work, to really refresh and invigorate you. You can use this time to take a short walk or to make a cup of coffee or tea. Whatever you choose to do, you must get up and leave the computer to do it. You cannot use your break time to check emails, Facebook, Twitter or your smartphone.

After you do four of these Pomodoro segments, you take a longer 15- to 30-minute break.

Reward Yourself

Once you've done the hard work your day held and accomplished all your action steps, it's time to reward yourself for your achievement.

Rewarding yourself is *extremely* important, particularly after you've stayed committed to achieving tasks in a given time frame and not allowed distractions or interruptions.

 Rewarding Yourself in Seven Steps

1. Take a half-hour break and relax. Meditate, read a book or take a power nap.

2. Go for a gratitude walk and take in all the wonders of nature. Express gratitude and appreciation for what you see, smell, hear and experience. You'll return to your office much more refreshed.

3. Treat yourself to a half-hour coffee break. Use a special creamer or coffee bean to give the break a touch of something special.

4. Have lunch or coffee with a good friend.

5. Allow yourself 15 minutes later in your day to visit your favorite fun forum or website or to play your favorite mindless video game.

6. Listen to some uplifting music from your happy playlist.

7. Write down your wins and victories in your Victory Journal or read over all those you've already recorded.

Chapter 8:

Coaching Yourself to Victory

Before we part, I want to give you a few more steps to aid your progress.

Procrastination: The Motivation Killer

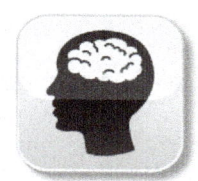 Procrastination is closely allied to indecision and being overwhelmed. Not dealing effectively with these feelings, as I've just covered, can result in procrastination, a form of inaction that's absolutely devastating.

Procrastination often uses your tendency for indecision as an easy out, an excuse for not doing anything. And just as positivity and negativity can build momentum in your life, so too can procrastination if you allow it to go unchecked. Here are seven steps to help you move that obstacle out of your way and continue forward.

 ## Overcoming Procrastination in Seven Steps

Ask yourself these questions and be totally honest with yourself when writing down your answers.

1. Why am I procrastinating? What are my underlying reasons?

2. What benefits am I getting from procrastinating?

3. What are the downsides of procrastinating on this project/task?

4. What would the benefits be if I moved forward and crunched through my procrastination on any given topic?

5. What is the first step I can take to stop procrastinating?

6. What are some tools I can use to stop the particular procrastination distraction I'm indulging in? For example, if you procrastinate by surfing the Web, you can install a Web-blocking program such as Cold Turkey or turn off your Wi-Fi.

7. What small goals can I set in order to help motivate me to stop procrastinating?

The Imperfection of Perfectionism

Perfectionism, indecision and procrastination are all related. Each freezes you in your tracks, halting progress completely.

Perfectionism leaves us so afraid to make a mistake or come up short of our idealized vision that we can't finish anything at all. Perfection is unachievable, and the quest for something impossible makes it easier to procrastinate or give up entirely.

At the end of the day, it's just more excuses. Nothing you do has to be perfect. The true tragedy is not when things get done and have small flaws—it's when they don't get done at all.

You'll feel elated when you finish something and then just let it go. The high feeling and experience of doing the task will motivate you to do more. It's like an adrenaline rush when you see that you've actually accomplished what you thought was impossible.

Messes and Incompletion

A mess is any incomplete task, obligation or unresolved commitment. Anything you've left incomplete will nag at you and create additional stress in your life.

Clutter is also a mess. Clutter takes up valuable space while stagnating energy, efficiency and creativity. It leaves little or no room for new, positive energy to flow. Regularly declutter your home, office and garage.

Think of each mess as a program running on your computer, but in this instance, it's running in your brain, creating confusion, chaos and eventual overload. As a result, everything's working slower and is scattered all over the place.

 Completing Projects and Cleaning in Seven Steps

1. Make a list of your messes and incomplete tasks or projects.

2. Rearrange the tasks in order of importance.

3. Break down the list even further by moving tasks into associated groups, if possible. This will allow for better efficiency as you can focus on like tasks together.

4. Assign a timeline with dates for starting each task.

5. Create a second timeline denoting the proposed date for each project's or task's completion.

6. Set a separate weekly timeline for decluttering your spaces. The initial declutter could be a big deal, so be sure to focus on one space or one corner of a space at a time—maybe even one cupboard, filing cabinet or drawer. Make it simple, and then it will be less daunting to attack the problem. Your weekly updates should be to maintain that decluttered space.

7. Note your wins and victories in your Victory Journal.

Comfort Zone or Confinement Zone?

 We all like to be comfortable, safe and cozy. It's human instinct. But when that gets in the way of trying new things or taking bold action steps, it can be debilitating and will cut you off from achieving your next goal.

The Value of Moving Beyond Your Comfort Zone

You can't ever know all that you're capable of if you never test yourself. You'll turn down countless opportunities as you try to remain inside your cocoon of safety. Sadly, this cocoon doesn't actually keep you safe—it actually keeps you vulnerable. It limits your resources when times get tough and restricts the scope of your skills because you haven't allowed yourself to develop any skills outside the zone.

Once you do stretch a little, the resulting adrenaline rush will embolden you to try more. It's a desensitizing process. Moving incrementally outside of your comfort zone, extending your abilities a little bit at a time, results in significant successes for you, leaving you invigorated with a satisfying sense of achievement.

Breaking Out of the Comfort Zone in Seven Steps

1. Select a small step you can take that will stretch you outside of your comfort zone. If it's just one step forward that helps you dip your toe in the water, it'll be easier to accomplish and that victory will lead to more.

2. Keep the momentum going by thinking of further small steps that build upon one another to gain even more momentum.

3. As you master the small steps, identify a bigger step to take.

4. Record each move beyond your comfort zone as a victory in your Victory Journal.

5. Share the move you made beyond your comfort zone with an accountability partner, in your mastermind group, or with a positive, supportive friend.

6. Write down each new opportunity, skill or benefit that comes from a move outside your comfort zone.

7. As you find yourself taking additional steps out of your comfort zone and you see the positive results, tweak your plans accordingly.

Chapter 9:
Maintaining Ongoing
Motivation

Your Victory Journal is a major tool in maintaining motivation. It has the power to inspire you as you read over your past wins and see how far you've come, and it holds you accountable when you commit to writing in it every single day.

Imagine the day you write in your Victory Journal but have no wins to share. It probably feels awful just thinking about it. The fact that you never want that to happen will mean you're always searching for the means to create a victory every single day. And what is the easiest way to create a victory? It's to be positive when you approach your various tasks.

Capitalizing on the Snowball

Your positivity snowball is another aspect of the positive edge that will keep your motivation from flagging. As the snowball of positive energy attracts more and more opportunities and good things to it, you'll become less likely to abandon the process. The way that positive energy makes you feel and changes your life is addictive—you'll want to make sure you continue getting those happy feelings and endorphins.

In the beginning you may struggle to remain positive when you're used to allowing yourself to be negative. But over time, positivity will become more than just a habit. It will become an impulse and an automated reaction akin to breathing.

Using Affirmations to Boost Your Mood

In the beginning of this book, we talked about self-limiting beliefs and how a focus on these beliefs can be detrimental to your progress. The key to beating your self-limiting beliefs and maintaining your motivation and dedication to the positive edge is to focus on your daily uplifting affirmations. These affirmations give you powerful statements to dwell on that center around positivity. They help you identify your intense strengths and they keep you reaching for that ideal life.

When you're going through a tough time, affirmations can help retrain your brain and subconscious into focusing on positive messages instead of negative. Be sure to repeat your affirmations in a strong voice both in the morning and in the evening before you go to bed so that you give your conscious brain and your subconscious brain the best opportunities to integrate these messages into your attitude.

Accountability Partners and Coaching: Motivation Squared

Working with an accountability partner offers a great way to commit to what you intend to achieve and keep yourself on track. It creates a like-minded camaraderie, and the interaction and feedback offers a valuable learning experience.

Finding an accountability partner is easy. It can be a very positive, supportive, nonjudgmental friend, or someone you have connected with in a recent group or online.

Think about whom you could connect with as an accountability partner, and contact them.

You can also form or join a mastermind group. This is like having an accountability partner but magnified because you have the power and support of a group of six to 12 like-minded people. Each mutually encourages and guides others to achieve their individual goals and dreams.

Each person brings his or her own distinct strengths, skills and expertise to the group. Support is given in a nonjudgmental environment that encourages everyone to feel free to contribute and bring out the best in themselves. You can take your projects to be critiqued or commented upon, and to seek additional input, ideas and specific skills or expertise.

The power of the combined energy and talents of the mastermind group is undeniable. Each contribution opens your eyes to a new viewpoint and insight. You will come away enriched and having learned new insights, actions and methods.

Coaching offers another way to not only get and stay on track with your goals but to help discover why you have trouble doing so in the first place. A good coaching program will help you discover both good and bad traits about yourself that you didn't even know you had. A coach can then tailor his or her advice to your specific situation and help you get on the right path—and stay there.

If you put the work in, you won't have trouble maintaining the positive edge. If you're determined to live your ideal life, once you start seeing the rewards that the positive edge lifestyle puts in front of you, you won't want to let go of the hope that this process gives.

Chapter 10: Congratulate Yourself

Congratulations! You've completed the first step in your journey to a new life—one with the positive edge. The next step is to take the positive edge principles and push them further. Apply them to more areas of your life. Develop and refine them so that you may advance along your personal development journey.

Remember this core truth and you absolutely cannot fail: the positive edge is all about maintaining action over the long term and taking repeated steps forward until your new, positive habits become automatic.

This is the end of the book, but it's not the end of your adventure. You've only just begun exploring the true depth of the positive edge.

I sincerely hope you've enjoyed your time here as much as I've enjoyed sharing these principles with you. I trust you've found the concepts and elements empowering and the practical seven-step action plans helpful and easy to integrate into your daily life.

Working through the book, you now see that the positive edge isn't just about a positive attitude on its own. It's about creating a holistic, integrated attitude and action system that reinforces your objectives and helps you become who you want to be.

By now, you should be well on your way to creating a daily habit that supports your transformation into your idealized self. Dedicate yourself to applying these lessons consistently, and over time you'll notice that your thought patterns, habits, behaviors and actions begin to take on a positive life of their own. You'll create new neural pathways and see practical changes manifest every day.

As time progresses, you'll find that you automatically see everything more positively. You'll also notice the law of attraction working and more positive things happening to you.

Finally, you'll see, as you review both your life and Victory Journal, that you're achieving what you set out to do. You're connecting and networking with new people and a wonderful world of opportunities will start to appear.

I am so excited for you! You're well on your way to achieving the life of your dreams—your positive edge life. Treasure that life, maintain it and never go back to your old way of being.

DESIGNING YOUR LIFE

What would happen if you discovered you could do more than just live your life—you could *design* it? This book teaches you to harness the power of your subconscious and program it to help you live a happy life fitting your definition of perfection.

DESIGNING YOUR LIFE: ACTION GUIDE

These exercises help you master your subconscious, abolish negativity and raise self-esteem. This guide focuses on creative visualization and powerful affirmations, to control your life's design and master your future.

DEVELOPING PERSEVERANCE

A combination of internal roadblocks are holding you back, preventing you from persevering. This book shows you how to break through these self-imposed obstacles to begin moving along your true path, taking you further than you ever thought possible.

DEVELOPING PERSEVERANCE: ACTION GUIDE

With this guide, you'll learn about the unique roadblocks you've designed for yourself and explore the thoughts, feelings and events that impact your ability to succeed.

YOU DESERVE TO BE RICH

If you're busy blaming your lack of wealth on upbringing, education and environment, you're missing out on learning how easy it is to get rich. This book teaches you to throw away the excuses and focus on the 12 steps to securing a future of financial success.

YOU DESERVE TO BE RICH: ACTION GUIDE

You deserve an ideal life. This workbook helps you get there by providing activities and strategies that explain the rules of greatness, help define your dreams and work to banish your fears.

UNLEASH YOUR MOJO

You already possess everything you need to be the person you want to be, you just have to access these powerful traits. In *Unleash Your Mojo*, you'll learn to recognize all the greatness inside you and discover how to put it to use and start living your ideal life.

Unleash Your Mojo: Action Guide

Each of us has power to succeed yet many of us never tap into that power. Instead we stagnate on the sidelines while others flash forward in life. This workbook gives practical tips, advice and exercises to advance in your quest for authenticity and power.

The Positive Edge

There's a secret behind living a happy, successful, fulfilling life: *Positivity*. Learn how to overcome your tendency toward negativity, how to control your life and future, and how easy it is to improve your confidence and self-esteem.

Spark: The Key to Igniting Radical Change in Your Business

A complete, step-by-step training program to help you become a high performer and higher earner. Learn how to rise to the top of your profession, position yourself as an expert and attract the abundance you desire.

DARE TO SUCCEED

Get the motivation and the information you need to rise to the next

level of success! America's #1 Success Coach, Jack Canfield, has gathered together the top business minds in one powerful book. This guide contains their secret strategies to conquer the competition and bring ongoing abundance into your life.

VICTORY JOURNAL

The *Victory Journal* demonstrates the importance of writing down all your daily wins. Inside you'll find exercises to help define your ideal self and create action steps to move closer to your goals.

HARNESSING THE POWER OF GRATITUDE

Recognize the positive energy moving through your day and harness it with this undated journal. Filled with inspirational quotes to help you maintain the spirit of gratitude, it's an ideal tool for developing an enduring, powerful habit of thankfulness.

APPRECIATING ALL THAT YOU HAVE

This 365-day journal filled with inspirational quotes provides a safe space to write down the many things you're thankful for. It's the perfect way to help shift your perspective and recognize the abundance of positive forces in your life.

THE PSYCHOLOGY OF SALES:
FROM AVERAGE TO RAINMAKER

Take your sales from lackluster to rainmaker without any smarm, aggressive tactics or dishonesty. This book teaches sales pros the psychology of their customers so they can present products the right way for each shopper.

THE PSYCHOLOGY OF SALES: ACTION GUIDE

In this action guide, you'll gain greater insight into your own personality and psychological makeup as well as that of your customers so you can further your sales success and transform your career.

RETIREMENT YOU CAN'T OUTLIVE

Cut through the hype and challenge conventional wisdom with a book focusing on conservative and reasonable ways to save for retirement. This book uses plain language and lots of common sense that's been missing from financial planning sessions for decades.

RETIREMENT YOU CAN'T OUTLIVE: ACTION GUIDE

Transform the lessons taught in *Retirement You Can't Outlive* into action steps that change the shape of your financial future. This immersive tool contains worksheets, exercises and review sheets to help you develop a plan to rescue your financial future.

NAVIGATING THROUGH MEDICARE

Don't be confused by the rules, plans and parts of Medicare. This book simplifies the complex system and allows you to quickly and easily make the right decision for the future of your healthcare. It's a one-stop guide to everything you need to know.

AVOIDING A LEGACY NIGHTMARE

Poor planning can rip your estate from your loved ones. *Avoiding a Legacy Nightmare* is a simple guide to help you get started in creating an effective estate plan that achieves all that you intended.

PHYSICIANS: MONEY FOR LIFE

If you want to retire on your own terms, you must understand the special considerations that physicians need to make in order to maintain sustainable retirement plans. *Physicians: Money for Life* casts aside traditional advice that's not suited to conservative retirement planning and focuses on helping physicians design a plan that creates money for life.

PHYSICIANS: MONEY FOR LIFE: ACTION GUIDE

You have the knowledge necessary to change the financial health of your retirement, now it's time to apply it. This action guide helps you transform the lessons taught in *Physicians Money for Life* into action steps you can take to change the shape of your retirement. With worksheets, exercises and review, this guide will help you move forward in your retirement planning journey while devising a plan to save it.

ALZHEIMER'S LEGACY GUIDE

Alzheimer's patients and their caregivers face a race against the clock and must learn how to cement a well-thought-out legacy plan before the disease's mental, emotional and psychological effects start to take their toll. This book provides guidance to both the recently diagnosed and those who will care for them as the disease progresses.

FINANCING YOUR LIFE: THE STORY OF FOUR FAMILIES

This is the story of four families that took their financial lives out of the red and into the black. There's McKenna, a single mom of two boys, working hard every day as a waitress; Toby and Shannon, two professionals battling a layoff and personal spending demons; Blake and Christine, a newlywed couple in a hurry to start living the good life, whether they can afford it or not; and Marcie and Kurt, two  young parents struggling to keep up in an increasingly image-obsessed society.

FINANCING YOUR LIFE: THE FINANCIAL RECOVERY KIT

Financing Your Life is an innovative financial recovery kit devoted to teaching you how to take total control over your financial life. Within, you'll learn about the secret behind financial planning, budgeting basics, insurance, credit repair, getting out of debt, developing financial compromise with a spouse or partner, saving and investing, mortgages and more. This tool does more than just tell you about financial concepts; it helps you begin immediately integrating what you learn into your own financial life.

GOAL, PLAN, START: THE GPS PROGRAM

Every day, thousands of people seal their own fates by failing to write down their goals. With the Goal, Plan, Start (GPS) Program, you can learn how to identify what you want out of life — and get it.

With this kit, you'll learn how to set goals that are actionable, define your ultimate intentions, identify the various types of goals you have, track your progress and keep setting new challenges for yourself.